May God give you
Faith like
Fire!
Pat Owen
Matthew 7:7-8

Faith like Fire

Engulfed by a Great God

Pat Owens

CROSSBOOKS
PUBLISHING

CrossBooks™
A Division of LifeWay
1663 Liberty Drive
Bloomington, IN 47403
www.crossbooks.com
Phone: 1-866-879-0502

First published by CrossBooks 8/1/2011

ISBN: 978-1-4627-0539-9 (sc)
ISBN: 978-1-4627-0540-5 (hc)

Library of Congress Control Number: 2011934738

Printed in the United States of America

This book is printed on acid-free paper.

To Ray

You are without doubt, the most humble man
God ever created. You have influenced lives
far more than you will ever realize.

Most of all, mine.

To Kimberly

Your tender giving heart has always inspired me
and your talents are a gift to all who know you.

To Tim

Your willingness to always help and guide this computer
dinosaur has led me to believe I really could do this.

To Jonathan

You have been a shining example to me of
perseverance. While I persisted to write, you
too persisted to achieve your degree.

Together we celebrate the success of endurance!

For my Grandchildren

Clayton, Reece, and Sydney, you are the next
Owens generation. I knew of real happiness when
I became a mother. Now I know the incredible joy
of being your grandma. This book is for you.

Contents

Acknowledgements

This book would never have been completed without the great host of friends and family that have traveled this journey of faith alongside me. Your prayers and encouragement as well as your financial support of Faith Steps Ministries, have not only blessed me but also have surely made the Lord smile. My Sunday morning sisters in faith have often held me up in prayer and support during the times I grew weak. I owe Linda and Vicki a debt of gratitude for keeping me supplied with incredible gourmet coffee. Each chapter found its way into the hands of Karen, my incredibly keen-eyed editor. I couldn't have done it without you. Butch, you know the place you have held in my heart throughout all these years. Thank you for helping me write those really hard chapters and for keeping me focused on the One who truly is the author. You painting my toenails will always be the best memory!

The cover of a book is always the first impression. I have my daughter, Kimberly and my son, Tim to thank for using their gifts and talents to dress my words in such an incredible way. As the photographer and graphic designer, you both have made me immensely proud to have my book bear your names.

This book would never have told the extent of God's mighty work if it were not for those who have allowed me to share their stories. Foremost among them is my mother. She remains a shining example of God bringing beauty from ashes and restoring what the enemy sought to steal from us. God gave a very young woman five children and because she held to her faith throughout a difficult journey, I know a love I might never have known. I have my mom to thank for the unspeakable joy of sharing life and faith with my siblings, Bonnie, Debbie, Russell and Doug. This book could not have been written without your love and your prayers.

To Joyce and Richard I offer a heart of thanks for the many times you have allowed me to hide and find respite in your home. Your love and the times of prayer have nourished my soul and made me better able to complete what God has led me to write.

While some names in the book have been changed to allow for their privacy, I am eternally grateful that God allowed me the privilege of traveling my journey of faith alongside them. Daddy, David, Mike, and Phyllis have gone on to heaven before me, and I look forward to those great reunions. We won't truly know until then the great extent to which God will have used our story. I pray that they will each be honored just as I seek to honor God.

Finally, I humbly acknowledge that because Jesus is Lord this book has truly been authored by Him. All glory is His!

Preface

How can faith be like fire? What exactly does that mean? Faith is something we place our belief and trust in. In fact, to believe or trust in somebody or something, especially without logical proof is exactly the belief Christians embrace. The Bible defines faith in Hebrews 11:1 as "the reality of what is hoped for, the proof of what is not seen." For the Christian, faith is a belief that God is real regardless of whether one can literally see him or not.

At first I came to believe in God because I was taken to church from infancy and taught to believe in Him. As I grew and heard all the incredible stories of the Bible, I began to understand that Jesus was someone who came to earth with an amazing purpose. Even more amazing was that his purpose involved me personally. I didn't fully understand, yet I realized it was true that he had lived here on earth and had died an undeserving death. His death was a sacrifice He made so that not only myself but all mankind could have a relationship with God. No other person did what Jesus has done for mankind because no one else has ever risen from the grave, conquering death so that we all might live forever with God. Why would anyone do that? The Bible states that it was because He loved us. John 3:16 states it this way, "For God loved the world in this way: He gave His One and Only Son, so that everyone who believed in Him will not perish but have eternal life."

Later, as I grew older I fully understood what God had done for me personally. I was included in the "everyone" of John 3:16. I entered into a relationship with God through believing and accepting the gift of life Jesus had given me. I could be forgiven of wrong things I had said and done, as well as the effect my poor choices had at times had on others. This began my faith journey. I had no way then of knowing how God would love and guide me. Sometimes the journey has been ecstatically fun while other times it's a barren drought. In other words, being in relationship with God doesn't mean that my life is perfect. What it does mean is that I always have God by my side and working for my good.

I came to realize that faith can often be confused with church membership or attendance. We can become entrapped in routine and tradition. I certainly did! When life brought about challenges, I didn't find that a mundane faith allowed me to truly experience the God I read about in the Bible. I wanted to know why God didn't display his greatness today as He did in the times of those Bible stories I read. I began to passionately pursue knowing God as personally as He would reveal Himself to me. _Faith like Fire_ tells the amazing story of my faith journey.

Fire is a consuming element. It is a force to be reckoned with. My faith truly became like fire. It burned away the dross of religion and its many encumbrances. Instead, faith became a force that brought purpose not only to the suffering but also to the wonderful things in my life's journey. It resulted in a story that needed to be told. Why tell it? Perhaps the greatest purpose is the potential to ignite another who desires to break free of religion and understand relationship with God. This truly is His purpose: that we know and experience His all-consuming greatness. To experience that is to be engulfed by a Great God.

Chapter One

The Value of Knowing God

When Life's Circumstances Tempt Us to Doubt

I remember little about the design of her casket or the colors of the flowers that blanketed it. Phyllis had always loved flowers. Her talent of arranging just the right flowering stems or budding blossoms outshined others. She seemed to know exactly the type of flower necessary to bring a bouquet to elegance. She was a woman possessing inner beauty that radiated throughout everything she did. Much like a delicate rose, she was one that appeared so beautifully and boldly yet lasted such a short time.

Our circle of friends had been woven through a tapestry of shared life experiences lasting nearly ten years. We came together somewhat by happenstance. One of us within our circle of friends had faced the sudden death of her husband. Through both the times of encouragement and support, we found that a bond was being formed. During those ten years we were strengthened in both the joys and the challenges each of us faced.

Regardless of the strength of our circle we were unprepared for the news that Phyllis' breast cancer had returned with a vengeance. It rocked us to our core, yet the bond we had already felt only deepened more and grew into something only God could knit together within our hearts.

Phyllis had fought breast cancer from the age of forty. She had celebrated being cancer free for five years and then with a crashing blow her cancer returned. Not only did she fight it but everyone who loved her fought it alongside her. The reports came that in spite of every available form of treatment she had endured, the cancer had now metastasized to her liver. It was devastating news for all of us. We encircled her with prayer and fought against this enemy while entreating every force God could bring against her disease. Mercy given to us from our God, in response to prayer, gave us four more years with her. These were years filled with episodes of despair but many times we were able to share laughter and true sisterhood.

Ironically we had dubbed ourselves with the title of *Mercy Sisters*. The name was chosen because none of us felt we exhibited a great deal of mercy. We were all women who didn't mind telling it as we saw it. If we felt one of us needed correction we would often jokingly say, "I'm going to slap you in the name of Jesus!" God's mercy had given her to us longer than any doctor expected and now those who had come to be known as the *Mercy Sisters* bid farewell to her just weeks before her fiftieth birthday.

As the four of us exited the church funeral service, my eyes moved to the pew we had sat in week in and week out. My tears blurred those who now occupied that pew. The memories however, of us worshipping hand in hand and praising our God for great things He had done were seared in my mind. She died on a Monday, only missing one Sunday in worship. Now hand in hand each of us, all sisters in heart, followed in procession behind her casket as we exited the church. With crushing grief, we passed the pew where never again would we be hand in hand with her. It seemed unbearable to imagine.

Once inside the car and hidden from the crowd, our sorrow caved in as we wept upon one another's chest. The long chain of cars slowly moved in an almost silent rhythm turning from street to street. It was a mute song of testament to Phyllis' intense passion for the good of all who had been touched by her caring heart. Life without her advice and unconditional love seemed beyond our understanding. At the cemetery, cars sat motionlessly, silence reigned, and time stood still in reverence for the gentle placing of her casket at the graveside. A courageous warrior in a battle she had been determined to win, she was now silent and gone from us. She was more than a friend; she was a sister. Though not born into the same family, the five of us could be no closer. It was a bond that God Himself had formed and now He had severed it. Together we wept as both our circle and our hearts felt broken.

Where is God when a loving, trusting soul is seemingly snatched away? How does one reconcile the love of God taught and embraced by Christians with the seemingly unfair circumstances of life? When hearts are ripped by crime, disease, or catastrophic events, how does one continue to embrace a belief in a God who by biblical description is defined as love? There are times when God doesn't intervene and alter the circumstances that appear to have no meaning. Certainly many have abandoned their faith during these times.

When my friend Phyllis died at the age of forty-nine, I had already begun to search for the answers to these and many other questions about God. Having been taken to church as an infant, I really knew no other way of spending Sunday other than attending church. Becoming a Christian in my teens and later marrying a man preparing to work in full-time ministry, I discovered I had conditioned myself to relate the experiences of my faith to my church attendance. When I was younger, I felt it was all about being at church, participating in programs, and living in a way that pleased those who attended alongside me. I didn't fully grasp the meaning of a personal relationship with God until much later.

> The character of God doesn't change in response
> to my circumstances. His character remains
> steadfast and is always trustworthy.

My story is no doubt woven with the same threads of intriguing questions countless others have asked. Many have served faithful lives in the church only later to find they confronted circumstances in which God's love seemed distant or even worse, non-existent. The account of my journey of faith is shared not with the intent of simply telling it. It is instead written for those who find themselves in the midst of their walk of faith, encountering experiences which storm upon the beliefs and teachings of all they have believed God to be. It is for those who desperately desire to hold on to their faith in the worst of times; even in those times where the injustice of life seems to reign and we are tempted to wonder if God is truly aware of our struggle. It is those times when we embrace the truth that our circumstance doesn't change God's character. In choosing to believe this, I am drawn into a deeper understanding of God's trustworthiness and ultimately, I experience a deeper relationship with Him.

My story is shared from the viewpoint of a fellow traveler upon this journey of faith. It is the account of a child who simply believed what she had been taught about God. It wasn't until a few raging tides of loss and despair swept in upon my orderly household of faith that I had need to question. Did God's love hold firm in the midst of these storms? If so, where could He be seen in the suffering, and if He could not, what value was there in believing? This account of my faith journey is for those willing to confront hard questions they perhaps ponder but are too afraid to ask.

What is the value in asking? It is as The Bible calls it, the pearl of great price.[1] In the book of Matthew, the kingdom of heaven is said to be like a merchant who searches for fine pearls. This merchant is not one who settles for just anything, but rather he wants the prize pearl. When he finds it, he is willing to sell everything he has to obtain it. Recognizing what Jesus did for each of us when he freely gave his life upon the cross as payment for the debt of sin, I understood that in this parable Jesus was this prize pearl. I also recognized my inability to sell anything in order to obtain it. Yes, I may be willing to sell everything in order to have it, but I also knew that no possession anyone had could measure in value to Christ's sacrifice. His death upon the cross was freely given as a gift of his love and obedience. I simply had to accept this gift. I could not barter nor could I purchase it. No amount of wealth, service, or acts of kindness could be offered in exchange for that which Jesus offered freely.

As one who had grown up in the Christian faith and been taught the meaning of Christ's death, I had to question if I truly had the passion this merchant exhibited. Did I place the kind of value on my relationship with God and my ultimate home of heaven that this merchant did? It was easy to give a resounding "Yes" and even nod with an "Amen" when all was going well. In times of blessing or abundance we often shower accolades on God and thank Him. We don't question His motives or His gifts. We speak of His goodness sometimes in direct correlation to the goodness of our existence. How often when life is challenging or even downright miserable, do we speak of Him with those same accolades?

Perhaps you too have often enjoyed songs of God's goodness and basked in the promise of His presence at all times. As the journey of my life began to have challenges that seemed contrary to God's goodness, I began to rethink my attitudes about how I viewed God. I had seen countless others who had walked away from relationships when the going got tough. I had even witnessed a few who chose to walk away from God.

---

1   "Again, the kingdom of heaven is like a merchant in search of fine pearls. When he found one priceless pearl, he went and sold everything he had, and bought it." Matthew 13:45-46 HCSB

When I began to question my deeply held beliefs about God, it came out of a desire to find answers rather than simply abandon my beliefs and my relationship with The Lord. I valued my church. I valued the decision I had made earlier in life to accept the Bible as truth, and I believed that God was who He claimed to be. Often I would find myself singing in worship, exalting God as One who is good all the time. Either I wanted to believe unreservedly that God was indeed good all the time, or I wanted to stop singing the song. Confronting this challenge to my beliefs brought me to a deeper walk of faith, which would ultimately be defined by great experiences with God.

Does The God of our Universe need my story told in order to justify Himself? Certainly not! It's not a question of need. Instead, He chooses to use our stories of faith to proclaim to others that He truly is a God who can be trusted. In telling my story, I pray He receives the glory He so deserves. My prayer is that He would use these words written from my heart to perhaps encourage another who struggles with the difficulties our journey upon this earth can offer. I share my story because I have traveled a journey of faith and discovered Him in ways I never dreamed possible. Perhaps you will be challenged to understand more deeply the relationship He desires to have with you. I pray you will be passionately stirred to refuse to accept mundane faith. My desire is that you truly experience God and have your faith come to life. You can walk with the powerful God who loves and desires that we truly know Him. My adventurous discovery came because the more I chose to seek Him, the more I found Him.

Perhaps you find yourself as a fellow traveler who has felt the oppressive doubt that the difficulties and sadness of life can produce. Have you clung to your faith in desperate times of injustice or inexplicable circumstances? Perhaps even now you hang on silently while remaining in church, but you do not truly understand God's purposes. If you felt you could look into the face of God and ask out loud, "Who are you, and why do you choose to do as you do?" what do you imagine His response would be to you? Thankfully, I have learned that He is anxious, even searching for those who aren't afraid to ask and will take Him seriously. [2]

God welcomes the pursuit of wisdom and understanding.

---

2   "Now if any of you lacks wisdom, he should ask God, who gives to all generously and without criticizing, and it will be given to him." James 1:5 HCSB

There is, however, an important point to be made. There is a distinct difference between doubting and asking. To doubt is to exhibit distrust. The Bible contrasts wisdom and doubt in the book of James. We are encouraged to ask God for wisdom. The wisdom spoken of in this text is knowledge and understanding. It does not exhibit distrust as doubt does. Instead, it exhibits a desire to gain insight and to discover the inner qualities of our God. This is why the Bible encourages us so often to seek wisdom. We do this because it is in this way that we gain insight into the character of our God.

James follows with instructions to ask God for wisdom with a warning that we ask without doubting. He likens the doubter to a raging sea tossed about by the wind.[3] He further states that the doubter cannot expect to receive anything from the Lord.[4] Clearly we must establish the intent of our asking for this wisdom. Once we reconcile the intent of our desires with the established parameters of God's Word, then we enjoy a whole new level of freedom in our relationship with God. This relationship becomes much more personal and real to us. My experience of faith and the relationship I have developed with God grew out of the understanding of what it meant to seek wisdom. It meant that I could earnestly and without doubt, believe that I would gain insight and knowledge about God if I simply asked Him for what I believed He was willing to give to me.

I am, as you might be, an unrecognized believer. There are many of us in our busy world. We move about daily in the workplace, at the grocery, waiting at the ATM machine, or serving you at your favorite restaurant. We quietly live out our faith throughout the week as we worship, support, and participate in our churches and our communities. We live each day, often unknowingly, in the embracing arms of God's love and provision. Do we ever ask ourselves, "What makes our walk with God have any significance on those we pass daily in this journey of life?" Do we live out our faith in God simply to benefit us and to gain what we receive out of it? Can we say that we live for the purposes God has for our life or does our faith only benefit us? It can become so easy for our relationship with God to become defined by selfish personal interest being fulfilled. Have our numerous Bible studies and church activities driven us to deeper faith and greater service to God, or have we simply enjoyed it for our own benefit?

---

3   "But let him ask in faith without doubting. For the doubter is like the surging sea, driven and tossed by the wind." James 1:6 HCSB

4   "That person should not expect to receive anything from the Lord." James 1:7 HCSB

In fact, could it be possible to even weave our self-focused interest into our faith with such subtleness that we truly believe we are fulfilling both our purposes and God's with no real accountability? We may become a part of Bible studies, discipleship classes, or biblically-based groups because others are involved and we simply want to be a part of the group. Perhaps we receive recognition or in some way our self-worth is validated by saying we have experienced the same things others have experienced. The purpose of Bible study should always be to grow in our wisdom but it never stops at this pursuit. We should carefully examine the motivation and purpose for our desire to gain wisdom. This quest always has more to do with God than it does us. As we grow in our wisdom we also grow in our love relationship with God. The ultimate outcome leads us to service within both the church and our community.

This is what Jesus meant when he once looked to the apostle Peter and asked him, "Do you love Me?" Peter was like many of us in his response. He forthrightly exclaimed, "Lord, you know I do." After all, what Christian wouldn't want to answer Jesus in that same way? He told Peter that if he loved him then, "Feed My sheep."[5] If the pursuit of wisdom has the ultimate goal of understanding our God, then the more we experience this growth the more we will experience His great love lavished upon us. The building up of this love relationship should motivate us to serve Him and to feed the many sheep.

So who are the sheep and where are they? They are all around us in our daily lives. As we share the good news of Christ with others both in our words and also through our actions, we begin to see others grow in the same relationship we have experienced with God. If our pursuit of wisdom is for any other purpose than for us to ultimately impact and benefit others, then something is wrong. If the wisdom gained does not produce the fruit of others coming to know Christ, we should feel compelled to question our intent for greater knowledge of God. In my own personal journey I had to not only ask myself some questions regarding my pursuit of truly knowing and understanding God, but I also had to humbly admit that my pursuit of Him was often self-focused.

---

5   He asked him the third time, "Simon, son of John, do you love Me?" Peter was grieved that He asked him the third time, "Do you love Me?" He said, "Lord, You know everything! You know that I love You." "Feed My sheep," Jesus said. John 21:17 HCSB

God uses the experiences of my life to reflect
His character as He lives in me.

Entering into a personal relationship with God through His son,
Jesus Christ begins a faith walk. This journey continues as we live out
the relationship we have with Him. Our walk of faith with its many
experiences has purpose beyond our desires and pleasures being fulfilled.
As we see and recognize the one and only sovereign God who chooses to
indwell His presence in us, we become a mirrored reflection of our God.
The reflection of His character becomes our character, and others begin to
see God in ways that perhaps they never have before. My life experience
brought about events that seemed to allow God the opportunity to use
the example of my faith and His presence to show Himself to others who
might never have understood what real faith looked like.

When my life got hard, I realized I needed to better understand the
ways of my God. I wanted to be able to understand how He was working
even when it seemed difficult to believe he was there. If I were going to be
able to identify Him as love, a characteristic I had been taught He was,
then I knew I had to understand why there were times He seemed absent.
If He were the loving and powerful God I read about in scripture, then why
did He not seem to intervene and alter circumstances in ways that seemed
reasonable to me? I felt that if He were going to make any difference at all
in my life then I needed to better understand all He felt I was capable of
knowing about Him.

God can be held responsible for every truth taught
and every promise He has given in His Word.

The Bible tells us that in the beginning there was the Word and that
the Word became flesh and took up residence among us.[6] Jesus is the
Living Word. This makes God's Word, our Bible, so much more than
simply printed words. It is the divine, living revelation of God. To embrace
this truth was for me, the beginning of truly taking Him at His word,

6   In the beginning was the Word, and the Word was with God, and the Word was
    God. John 1:1
    The Word became flesh and took up residence among us. We observed His glory,
    the glory as the One and Only Son from the Father, full of grace and truth. John
    1:14 HCSB

and realizing that He could be held responsible for the truth of all that He says.

Holding God responsible was not to place myself equal alongside Him, as though He owed me explanations. Certainly, that wasn't the goal. I had met countless other Christians who had abandoned their faith when they found themselves confronting circumstances they could not accept or reason out with their own understanding. My search for answers and accountability from God came out of a desperate need to prove Him in my life rather than abandon Him. When I couldn't explain how He could be at work in circumstances, it was the searching for truth that drew me into a deeper understanding of Him. This pursuit became foundational in learning to walk by faith and give Him my complete and unwavering trust. If I honestly believed that God's Word was His truth living and at work in me and that this truth did not change, then I was accountable before God to exhibit an unwavering faith that was not dependent on my situation. This accountability in my relationship with God enabled me to begin to view myself as the mirrored image of Christ living in me. That mirrored image of Christ was not dependent upon any ability or endeavor on my part. Instead it was totally the surrender of my own will, in order to allow God His rightful place. It was simply admitting to Him that I was willing to surrender control. I wanted to know that all I had heard and learned of Him could not only be believed but also experienced.

This journey of faith brought me out of a powerless life in Christ into a walk of faith that ultimately became life-altering. What a relief it must have been for God to finally have me ask, "Truly, who are you? And what difference will it make in the events of life if I have embraced your love?" These questions were not asked out of foolish pride, but rather because I truly wanted Him to make a difference with my life. I wanted to honestly experience the value of knowing him.

There were times when I didn't understand how God was working. In the worst of times He seemed silent when I felt He should be heard. The choice for me was to either walk away or remain loyal in pursuit of proving the relationship. I chose the latter. It was not always an easy, clear choice. I struggled often in allowing God to reveal Himself and grow His love relationship with me. I became frustrated at times with myself. While I wanted all of God, I also had working within me, a selfish will to desire things that were contrary to God. Different events in my life allowed God the opportunity to reveal different characteristics of His love. Thankfully, He doesn't give up on those He love's.

I came to see that He had a true desire for me to know Him on His terms rather than my own. After all, He knew it would be life altering for me. He also knew that I would come to understand I had not trusted in a God still buried in a tomb but in one who was living, active and dependable. I would discover the God who was true to His word and could be held accountable for every description given of Him and every promise He had made. If He and I were to have a personal relationship that had any real purpose, there were things about Him I needed to know. There were also things I believe He was anxious to share. Isn't that exchange what a true love relationship involves? Certainly it is and it has less to do with church membership and more to do with experiencing God.

With different events came the challenge over and over again to either believe Him or walk away and miss other amazing scenes in this journey of faith. It is an unbelievable story. This journey is filled with amazing accounts of lives that impacted mine. They are stories of lives forever changed by the God who allows us to have times when we question and search to find Him. His promises are for those willing to not abandon their faith but instead seek Him with all their heart. When we pursue Him in this way, we will indeed find Him.[7]

While gathered among a throng of those who grieved at the grave of my friend Phyllis, I slowly moved away from the crowd. I watched as scriptures were read and prayers were offered. I heard consoling words wafting over the soft cries of so many whose lives had been touched by her caring way. My thoughts drifted to the night before when we had stood beside our friend's cold and lifeless body lying peacefully upon satin blanketing. Even in the midst of our agonizing grief we broke through tears into laughter. We had realized she was the only person we knew who had received an enormous bouquet of flowers sent from her dry cleaner. She had touched so many people in such loving, caring, and personal ways that even the dry cleaner recognized her passing. Together we felt her smiling spirit as we each made a pact with one another that when another of us should part in death, we would send an arrangement with condolences from the dry cleaner.

Now as I stood at her graveside, gazing out on this crowd, I knew there were many who asked the same questions I had once asked. How could a

---

7   Keep asking, and it will be given to you. Keep searching, and you will find. Keep knocking, and the door will be opened to you. For everyone who ask receives, and the one who searches finds, and to the one who knocks, the door will be opened. Matthew 7:7-8 HCSB

loving God find any purpose in taking one our world desperately needed? Throughout that large crowd I knew there were probably those who were being challenged in their faith. Then it was as if heaven opened its gates to allow us in the midst of a great cloud to see the light of heaven pour out. Sunlight suddenly broke forth through a gray sky, and I was reminded that the cloud of our day with all the unanswered questions did not mean God was not in our midst. I had learned this over many years, and this was by far, not the first unfair grave I had stood beside. I am certain that though He was unseen, The Lord walked with us behind Phyllis' casket, and he held us close in the car as we sobbed. When all seemed lost, He was present. Silent and unseen, but present nonetheless. I say this with complete certainty because I have learned it is true. As I returned home that evening, covered with a heavy blanket of loss, I lay silently in bed remembering another casket that had prepared me for this day. It was long before I knew God as I know Him now. Come along with me as I share my journey of embracing God.

Chapter Two

Simply Asking

How to Begin a Real Faith Journey

Real faith in God begins when we come to the end of all
our attempts at religion and simply ask to know God.

It is true that in this world we will encounter things for which there seem
to be no answers. There are no justifiable reasons. Ask anyone who has
exited the church behind the casket of one they love or buried the body
of one whose life has ended prematurely or unexpectedly. Talk to the one
who has experienced an illness or accident that altered their way of life.
Spend some time on the cancer floors of any children's hospital and you
will certainly see innocent faces. Life can be unfair and at times seem to
have no purpose. Even people with deep faith find there are times when
they must search to the depths of their souls to hold fast to their God in
the midst of life.

Have you too questioned or searched for God? Have you wished at
times that you could rewind time and alter circumstances? I once had a
friend in childhood who hated to lose at a game. Her way of never losing
was to suddenly rearrange the pieces of the game. When I encountered the
unfair times in my life, those times became a test of my belief system. It
was during these times I had to decide what my faith really was and how
it affected my outlook. It was so easy for me to assume that because my

circumstances had changed, God had changed as well. During these times it was easy to fall into a trap of doubting or blaming God.

I have determined that challenging times in my life can serve as opportunities to either weaken or strengthen my walk of faith. Regardless of the circumstances I may face throughout life, one thing is certain: the challenging times of my life are an opportunity for me to better define who my God is and how I see Him working in my life. This understanding of who God is and how He works was not an automatic outcome of my belief in Him. The relationship I had with God as I walked through challenging daily experiences led me to grow in my understanding of His character. I began to understand that God would remain the same no matter what the situation I may confront. As I saw that God was and always is the same loving, forgiving, and caring father that He professed through His word to be, I grew in trust and dependence on those identity traits.

The circumstance surrounding the events of my
life will not alter the character of my God.

The Bible defines God as love.[8] He is love at all times, even in the midst of what appears to be abandonment or silence. His love is not based upon what we can understand. It is based upon God Himself. It wasn't until I could grasp the magnitude of this truth that I realized not only the value of knowing Him, but also the great value He placed on me. His love was not confirmed by my sense of His presence in the circumstance. Neither was it confirmed by my ability to see how He was working. Either I believed He was completely in control of everything or I didn't. I had to settle this truth early on, or I would never have held to my faith during the years that would lie ahead.

My name is Pat. I am the second child in a family with four other siblings. I was born in Richmond, Virginia, to a mother who was 18 years old and who eventually had five children by the age of 22. It was during these young years of my mother's life that both she and my father became Christians. My father, who was 12 years older than my mother, ran a dairy route early on Sunday mornings. My mother would walk us to church as babies filling one large carriage while a couple of us toddled along beside her. It must have been an insurmountable task to get us all ready. Surely,

---

8   And we have come to know and to believe the love God has for us. God is love, and the one who remains in love remains in God, and God remains in him. I John 4:16 HCSB

there must have been times she walked that road questioning herself, "Do I even have *my* own clothes on?" It had to be so hard for her to persevere and recognize the importance of her work. Yet, I don't remember a time when church was not a part of our life. My father would later become a materials clerk for a large hospital in Richmond. He was then able to attend church with us regularly.

In those days, the church was a vital part of family life. There were not as many other things competing for a family's time as there are today. People were not racing to the gym, the video store, and countless children's activities and sports. It was truly a different way of life than we find ourselves living today. As a child, I sought to be involved in everything the church offered. If I was allowed to go, that's where you would find me. The distance of only two blocks enabled me to walk there if necessary, and many times that's exactly what I did.

During these formative years, I didn't yet understand that I had been born into a life planned by God, and that He was using this church and it's many programs and people to form a foundation I would later desperately lean upon. To me, church was a place of fun. It was a place that offered opportunities, friendships, and experiences I would have sorely missed if not there. During my childhood, the highlight of my summer was Vacation Bible School. It was a grand affair in which we all met with great enthusiasm outside the doors of the sanctuary. We would comb the lawn seeking our friends and gather with our age group. Each day children from the crowd would be chosen to carry the American flag, the Christian flag and the Bible. Each grade would march into the sanctuary to the sound of triumphal music playing from a pipe organ. As we followed these icons we held so dear, I learned to honor them and treat them with great respect. To this day, I savor the smell of peanut butter cookies because they remind me of snack time at Vacation Bible School. It was the one time during the year I got to drink a whole eight ounce soda from a glass bottle.

I grew up singing in choirs and participating in drama presentations. These became my earliest memories of learning how to feel confident speaking or performing before a crowd. Ladies would gather in the kitchen to prepare a meal for the youth choir on Sunday evenings. It would often consist of foods I didn't routinely have at home. Gathering with friends while sharing pizza and soda was a real treat for me. I certainly didn't realize at the time, the impact these experiences were having on my life. My involvement in programs and learning great portions of scripture became building blocks of my faith. At the time, I simply wanted to achieve and be recognized. I wanted to aspire to one level of learning in order to move on and attempt to conquer the next. Participating in everything, I sang in the choirs, joined in missions, and attended Bible studies. As an adolescent, I even enrolled in a study on the book of Revelation taught by my pastor. Though I probably didn't glean much from Revelation, a book I could hardly understand, I wanted to please everyone and desired to be found faithful even at a young age.

All of my striving to learn and to achieve ultimately led me to a place of understanding my need as a sinner for the love God had shown for me in Christ's death on Calvary. Though I sought to please others, I soon realized that no matter how good I tried to be or how much I sought to learn, I could not earn God's love. It had been given to me as a free gift through Christ.[9] I came to understand that even as a child I was in need of God's love and I realized that this was the only way to enter into relationship with God.[10] I remember hearing a Billy Graham crusade meeting being broadcast on television. I was in another room doing my homework and I listened intently as they explained how to pray and become a Christian. Even though I was only a fifth grader at the time, I knew that I wanted to pray that prayer. Sometime later I was ready to tell my pastor and my church about my prayer. Not long after that, I was baptized and with the heart of a fifth grader, I fully believed that I knew God. While I had no way of knowing God's plan for my life, it was the beginning of an incredible journey. Some years later, only a few feet away from where I had been baptized, I would exchange wedding vows at the altar of this same church.

> The circumstances surrounding my birth
> and my life experiences do not alter the
> truth that God has a plan for my life.

I met my husband Ray, who also grew up in this church and served as a part-time director of youth ministries throughout his college years. He believed God wanted him to make this his life's work. Following our

---

9   If you confess with your mouth, "Jesus is Lord," and believe in your heart that God raised Him from the dead, you will be saved. With the heart one believes, resulting in righteousness, and with the mouth one confesses, resulting in salvation. Romans 10:9-10 HCSB

10 Jesus told him, "I am the way, the truth, and the life. No one comes to the Father except through Me." John 14:6 HCSB

marriage, we moved out of state in order for him to attend seminary. This began my journey of coming to understand that I had been born into a life planned by God. Oh no, I certainly didn't recognize it at the time. It would take many more experiences to finally embrace this concept. Looking back, I now realize how important it was for me to understand that my life was planned by God. It was foundational in learning to live for God's purposes rather than my own.

For some people, the circumstances of their lives may not seem to lend evidence to the truth that we are planned by God and born for His purposes. God may not have seemed present in their conception or their lives, let alone actively pursuing them in love. I have shared time with many people as they expressed their doubts about God's activity in both their births and the years that followed in childhood. Some of these accounts would cause even the most devout follower of the scriptures to question if God had a plan and was in fact, in control. Yet, the psalmist acknowledged God was there when he was created inside the womb of his mother.[11] If I embrace this belief as the psalmist did, I must also believe there was a plan. My creation was not reckless and without thought.[12]

If this is true, why then are there birth defects? Why do some children who are created in the warmth and security of their mother's womb never see the light of life and instead enter the world still, silent, and without breath? It is somehow reassuring for us who are living in comfort to believe that God formed us and had an intentional purpose for us. How then are the parents of the child who lives in a vegetative state or the parents of a stillborn infant to be comforted? If our conceptions, births, and lives do not recklessly occur, but are planned by God, why then does He seem absent in circumstances that sometimes surround us? Did God somehow fail? Again, if He is a God of love, out of that love did He not value life in these circumstances? Did He sit by helplessly in conception and not intervene as He created? Or as He created the inward parts while knitting together the intricacies of the human body, could it be that He is somehow

---

11   For it was you who created my inward parts, you knit me together in my mother's womb. I will praise You because I have been remarkably and wonderfully made. Your works are wonderful, and I know this very well. Psalm 139:13-14 HCSB

12   My bones were not hidden from You when I was made in secret, when I was formed in the depths of the earth. Your eyes saw me when I was formless; all (my) days were written in Your book and planned before a single one of them began. Psalm 139:15-16 HCSB

responsible for the defect? These were questions that I ultimately found many were asking.

We recognize that birth defects, disease, and a host of other things were not a part of God's original plan for mankind. When sin entered into God's perfect creation, everything in our world changed. But does that mean He is powerless in these things? And if so, then where is the love of God? And in what way is that love expressed? Is this love understood by our definition or by His?

God's love and presence is not measured by circumstance.

When I began to study the book of Job, I began to understand God's definition of love was quite different from mine. His love was present whether I accepted it or not. Without question Job faced some difficult circumstances. He lost wealth, family and health. The loss and grief of one bad situation was only followed by another. Then, in addition to the loss, his friends gave unsolicited advice. Clearly Job had every reason to abandon faith in a God defined as love and yet he did not. I wanted to understand how he was able to do that.

In my own life, I began to realize the truth that neither His love nor His presence was measured by my circumstances. This was unlike my early church experiences in which I had learned to equate church attendance and involvement with relationship, love, and approval. Whether I experienced loss or gain, as Job did, God's character remained unchanged. He was and is always a God of love.

However, I must say, I delighted in discovering that Job questioned God.[13] He felt God was silent. Due to his circumstances, Job questioned if God considered him His enemy. Like Job, there were times I had felt this way about God. Perhaps you too have struggled at times wondering if you were somehow responsible for the outcome of your situation. You may have wondered if somehow through your behavior, your thoughts, or even your sin you may have become God's enemy. You may have even felt that you somehow deserved it. I had not always made right and good choices, and there were times I struggled with the thought that perhaps my circumstance was retribution for past sin.

In studying Job, I was most intrigued with God's ultimate response to him. When I found myself asking God, "Why?" as if His answer would justify His allowing my circumstances, I read how God responded to Job.

13 Why do You hide Your face and consider me Your enemy? Job 13:24 HCSB

I expected God to give an account for Himself. I was anxious to hear reasons and explanations why God would have allowed such adversity in Job's life. I somehow felt that if I could hear God vindicate Himself, I would understand Him more. God's response was anything but what I had expected. Instead of vindication or explanation, God questions Job by asking him, "Where were you when I formed the earth...?"[14] This was God's way of ultimately refining Job's perception of who God really is. I began to see that I too needed to refine my perception of God. Truly knowing Him became my passion.

Had I not begun this pursuit early on, I would have perhaps abandoned the greatest love I've ever known. When confronted with loss, suicide, and disease, all of which I ultimately faced, I would have let go of my faith because I felt I needed God's explanations. Truly, love doesn't mean we have all the answers. God's love cares for us as it presses on for the ultimate goal, even when the process is painful. What is the ultimate goal? It is that we truly know God through His son Jesus and that we fulfill His purpose for our days on this earth. This purpose has to do with our life here on earth but it also prepare us for eternity with Him. It is then that we shall see Him face to face and have full understanding of those things we don't or can't understand now. What seems to have been lost to us now, will be found. In the end, God restored what Job had lost.[15] It is the happy ending to the story. Did children born later replace the love in Job's heart for those he lost? I don't think so. I don't believe that was God's intent.

I do believe Job is for us a model of trust in times that make no sense. He is a model for us in times of unfairness, or for times when the doctor utters the words *malignant* or *incurable.* Jobs example is a source of encouragement when we are victims of tragic circumstances over which we have no control. It is direction for us who sit in the midst of unwarranted criticism, just as Job did while listening to ill-given advice from those he knew as friends. Ultimately it is the end of the story that gives us the greatest message.

The greatest message is not that Job received twice the number of animals, and wealth or that the same number of children was restored to him. It is not a score-keeping system in which God vindicates himself. The

---

14 Where were you when I established the earth? Tell (Me) if you have understanding. Job 38:4 HCSB

15 So the Lord blessed the latter part of Job's life more than the earlier. He owned 14,000 sheep, 6,000 camels, 1,000 yoke of oxen, and 1,000 female donkeys. He also had seven sons and three daughters. Job 42:12-13 HCSB

greatest message comes to us prior to Job's blessings. It is his understanding of God. Previously Job had based his understanding of God on what he had heard, and had been taught. Now he based that understanding on what he had learned through the circumstances he had faced.[16]

I questioned the love of God when I lost my first child during the pregnancy. It was during this time that the psalmist's words of God's involvement in creation took on meaning to me. If my life was valued in the creation process inside my mother's womb as the psalmist had declared, then was not the life of my unborn child? Was not this child equally valued in God's sight? Was God forming my child's "inward parts" as the psalmist described his own creation? I believed that He had formed mine with intent and purpose, then why not my child's? Had God somehow failed? Did my baby's life have no purpose? How could God be expressing love at the same time He allowed the healthy development of my baby to cease?

Ray and I wanted more than anything to love and nurture this child to grow in faith and understanding of who God was. We had married, finished school and felt we were in every way equipped and ready to become parents. We had a Christian marriage. We had answered God's call to serve Him full-time in ministry and had made many sacrifices in order to fulfill the educational requirements to equip us for ministry. We were now serving God full time and had established a Christian home. It seemed we had every justifiable reason in our lives for God to bless us with this child. I suppose I felt that because we desired to have children then God would naturally bring that about. It was crushing for me to believe that God would do otherwise. We had struggled with infertility for years and celebrated the pregnancy only to then find the hope of parenthood torn from us. How could God be seen as love through this? It was a question I could not resolve at the time.

There are times when God's purposes are fulfilled through suffering and loss. Jesus is our greatest example of this.

These early years of questioning led me to begin to understand my concept of God's love was very wrong. I did not come to this understanding easily or quickly. Over time and through experiences, I began to see that I had *all* of His love at both the times of receiving blessing and in times of loss. Again, I found solace and evidence of God's truth as I read in my Bible

---

16   I had heard rumors about You, but now my eyes have seen You. Therefore I take back (my words) and repent in dust and ashes. Job 42:5-6 HCSB

in the book of Job. It's a great story about unfair suffering. Job experienced loss when God allowed Satan to come against all that Job cherished. In losing land, possessions, wealth, and even children, one might ask, "Can a loving God allow such atrocities?" In my years of ministry I have met countless people who, out of their own life experiences, have asked this same question. Through Job's story I found evidence that God's love was not measured by what was given or what was taken. It had nothing to do with Job's accomplishments or achievements. God's love didn't rest on Job's definition of love but rather on God's. It was His love that sustained him and never left Job during his losses. It was quite often unseen, silent, and seemingly nonexistent. A purpose was being fulfilled through Job's suffering and loss In the end (and God had full control from beginning to end), Job knew the character of his God in a way he had not known and perhaps never would have come to know in any other way.

Satan felt that Job would abandon his faith if things were taken from him. Satan confronted God with this accusation. He proclaimed it was because God had allowed so much wealth, security, and comfort in Job's life that Job felt cushioned from any reason not to abandon his faith in God. Satan saw Job and Job's blessed life as a challenge to prove to God that His loving care for Job was nothing more than a safe hedge of protection. Satan claimed that this protection resulted in Job never questioning God's love.[17] Who of us might not have been tempted in the midst of such losses to curse God as Job's wife recommended he do? Yet, Job questioned, "Should we accept only good from God and not adversity?"[18] Here was evidence to me that Job was a man who had already begun to understand who His God was. Had it not been for God's presence, His sustaining love and the relationship he and God shared, Job may have succumbed to the temptation to abandon his faith as well.

God is still the same great and powerful
God we read about in His Word.

---

17   Satan answered the Lord, "Does Job fear God for nothing? Haven't you placed a hedge around him, his household, and everything he owns? You have blessed the work of his hands, and his possessions are spread out in the land. But stretch out your hand and strike everything he owns, and he will surely curse You to Your face." Job 1:9-11 HCSB

18   His wife said to him, "Do you still retain your integrity? Curse God and die!" Job 2:9-10 HCSB

In my own life I would yet face a few challenging circumstances and certainly wouldn't face them with the strength of Job's faith. Yet I longed to know God as Job did. When the testing of my faith came, I decided that the account of Job and so many others with great faith was evidence to me that I could risk believing that God is still that same powerful God and He is willing to do for me what He had done for them. While I struggled to understand how God could be working and why He chose not to allow me to conceive a child, I didn't want bitterness to cheat me out of a faith walk I was striving to pursue. In the worst of times I remember looking to the heavens with my Bible lifted up to Him and exclaiming, "I believe You are the same God today." I desperately wanted the kind of walk with Him I read about in the lives of great men of faith in The Bible. With that Bible extended to the heavens I exclaimed to God, "I believe I can know You as they did. Please let me walk with you and experience you in this way." Little did I know then the journey I had just begun. What I did know was that I was growing in my understanding of God and if I didn't want to abandon my faith, but instead wanted to truly know Him, I needed to simply ask.

Simply Ask Him

Simply ask Him, be not afraid.

Your debt of sin He's already paid.

Undeserving, you've come to believe?

Mercy and grace are free to receive.

Simply ask Him, your Father will give.

An abundant life He desires you live.

Do you need His power, desire His love?

Receive now freely from your God above.

Simply ask Him, He has paid at the cross.

You can know Him in greatness, even in loss.

Simply ask Him, no matter your pain

The power of His cross has become your gain.

Chapter Three

Sitting at the Well

The Risk of Caring for Broken Lives

The passionate pursuit to be led by God means
being willing to move as God moves, regardless
of personal sacrifice and with a deep conviction
that complete obedience is essential.

The Bible gives to us a wonderful account of Jesus as He positions Himself in the path of a broken life. It is found in chapter four of the book of John. Jesus had encountered the Pharisees' entrapping questions regarding His ministry. He did not debate but rather moved from one area to another in order to avoid confrontation with them. The opportunity for ministry to continue was more important than debating issues. Jesus did not let the questioning get in the way of the ultimate purpose of building the Kingdom of God. We would do ourselves a great service if we modeled Jesus' ability to walk away with complete trust that God is still in control.

To be used by God as an instrument to fulfill His purposes on earth, requires a willingness to be positioned in places that will offer service to others.

When Jesus left the area where He was being challenged, He knew that His father was able to carry on the work that had begun. Jesus traveled to Galilee with the express intent of doing that which He had been sent by God to do. In order to accomplish this, He found He must position Himself in a place where He would have the opportunity to minister. His example to us is one of being positioned and used by God in the everyday places where we encounter people. That example is seen as Jesus moved from the situation in John 4 and encountered a woman who desperately needed what only He could give her. In order for this woman to receive what Jesus offered, He had to position Himself in her path. He didn't wait for her to come to Him. She was an outcast who likely had a reputation for moving in and out of relationships with men. Women in her time would not have come to the well alone. They would have come in the fellowship of other women. Both her aloneness and the hour which she came were indicators that she did not want to be encountered by others. She had positioned herself at the well at that hour in order to avoid human contact and perhaps the ridicule or judgment that such contact would have brought upon her. You see, this is why so many whose lives are trapped in sin will not come to churches. They will position themselves away from the crowd because either they know or fear how they are regarded by others. Jesus, on the other hand, positioned Himself at the well at a time that afforded Him the opportunity to give her the hope of a new life. Similarly, God is always moving about, positioning Himself, in order to offer this hope-filled life. His desire is always to see the life trapped in sin to be set free.[19]

As Jesus positioned Himself at the well, He knew that she would find Him. The encounter with her was intentional. He had traveled on foot and was no doubt tired and thirsty. He used *His* need as the very means for meeting hers. He willingly positioned Himself not only in the *place* where she would be but also at the *time* she would be there. Christ modeled for us the qualities of willingness and availability. We may feel compassion regarding another person but that doesn't always lead us into a willingness to make ourselves available. The passionate pursuit to be led by God means being willing to move as God moves, regardless of personal sacrifice and with a deep conviction that complete obedience is essential. How often do we offer excuses for not being where God may use us because we base our inability to serve another on that which we believe we can or cannot do? In doing this we don't even give God the opportunity to show us His power at work in us.

---

19 "The Spirit of the Lord is on Me, because he has anointed Me to preach good news to the poor. He has sent Me to proclaim freedom to the captives and recovery of sight to the blind, to set free the oppressed, to proclaim the year of the Lord's favor." Luke 4:18-19 HCSB

How much more might God accomplish through us if we were more willing to leave our positions of comfort and become available in places of difficulty and insecurity? For most of us, this is a frightening prospect. Who of us hasn't felt at times a feeling of doubt regarding our own abilities? Perhaps you have heard yourself lament just as I have, "I could never do that!" We may find ourselves saying these very words while at the same time quoting Philippians 4:13, "I am able to do all things through Him who strengthens me." The idea of receiving strength and being able to do all things is appealing to us. We welcome that resource and many times consider it one of God's greatest promises. Yet we may not view it with the perspective of its entire purpose. The intent behind this great promise is given to us through the apostle Paul's writing in the verses that precede verse 13. He had learned to be content in whatever circumstances he found himself encountering.[20] Paul's contentment did not rest upon external factors or circumstances.

We may know a situation for which we truly believe that God is the answer to the need, yet the prospect of personal involvement may be something we resist. There is a distinct difference between knowledge of a need and involvement in meeting that need. Paul mirrored Jesus' example. He never stopped his involvement at the point of knowledge. He always sought to actively meet the need both personally and by involving others.

Originally, Paul had been a person who was literally hell-bent on destroying the purposes of Jesus' ministry. Then God did an amazing thing. He came on the scene of Paul's travels and the theologically well-educated Jew, who believed he was protecting the religion he had been taught, was transformed. Never again do we read of him questioning God's purposes for his life. He was fixed on fulfilling that purpose and did so at great cost. That is how he discovered the true message behind the promise of Philippians 4:13. He learned this by following the example Jesus gave. Like Paul, we have this same opportunity. As we position our lives for ministry we will see God work in ways we never could have imagined. It becomes an opportunity to see Philippians 4:13 lived out in our lives. Do you believe this is possible for you? Perhaps the first step to actually living

---

20 I don't say this out of need, for I have learned to be content in whatever circumstances I am. I know both how to have a little, and I know how to have a lot. In any and all circumstances I have learned the secret (of being content) – whether well fed or hungry, whether in abundance or in need. Philippians 4:11-12 HCSB

out the power of Philippians 4:13 would be to fully embrace the belief that it is possible.

> To fulfill any ministry opportunity where God leads
> will require a consistent acknowledgement that the
> power to accomplish this will rest in God alone.

The secret to fulfilling Philippians 4:13 and being able to "Do all things" is recognizing that it is not our power that accomplishes this. Actually, this becomes a great relief to the follower of Christ. If we thought that God had a purpose for our lives and left us here on Earth to fulfill that purpose without His active strength and power, then we would be a failure waiting to happen. Most often when I feel I have failed in an area of ministry it is because I have pursued it within my own strength. Sure. I may begin meeting a need with great enthusiasm but then grow weary with the demands. Even worse, I may become disillusioned because growth and success don't come quickly. This is where it becomes easy to lose sight of the truth that Christ is the source of strength and the power to bring about any real help or change.

While Christ in us produces the strength needed, we must never lose sight of another vital truth. Satan does not want God to succeed in using us in His Kingdom. The battle Satan wages in our lives has always been with God, not with us personally. He cares nothing for or about us personally. The Bible teaches us that his fight began with God when he sought to be as great as Him. He was catapulted from heaven as a defeated enemy whose only satisfaction now is to seek to destroy the lives of others and carry as many as possible with him to eternal damnation where he will suffer for all eternity.[21] No doubt, he sees any chance at destroying our lives, or ministry of a disciple of Christ, as his victory against God.

Because Satan is so cunning in his deception, he may even attempt to mislead us through the encouraging words of another believer. Satan may tempt us to receive these words and then begin to see our talents or abilities as the source of our power. Certainly it's a good thing both to give and

---

21 "Through the abundance of your trade, you were filled with violence, and you sinned. So I expelled you in disgrace from the mountain of God, and banished you, guardian cherub, from among the fiery stones." Ezekiel 28:16 HCSB

"The Devil who deceived them as thrown into the lake of fire and sulfur where the beast and the false prophet are, and they will be tormented day and night forever and ever." Revelations 20:10 HCSB

to receive praise. We all enjoy and thrive on encouragement and positive feedback. It's only when that feedback results in a prideful attitude that it becomes a danger to us. We do well to train ourselves to immediately acknowledge the work God has done through us. We must never lose sight of our complete poverty before God. When we daily humble ourselves before God, acknowledging that He knows all about us, we are reminded of the true person in the mirror. As we stand before a Holy God we are always in need of His grace, forgiveness and power. Others may look at us, hear our words, or see our activities and have a completely different picture of what God sees and knows about us. It is a place of complete humility to realize that in knowing all about us, God continues to love us and chooses to use us in His work. This is truly amazing grace!

People who are not living in relationship with God certainly go on to accomplish great things, both in life and also relationships. Just like the individual who is in relationship with God, they too face the mirror daily. Sadly, though, they are trapped at the mirror. They know their true inner self and recognize their success as well as their failures. Yet, even with their greatest accomplishments they are never able to experience authentic forgiveness for their failure. Only a relationship with God through Christ Jesus offers that.[22] Instead, they are trapped in a scorekeeping system within themselves. It can become a vicious cycle of trying to outweigh personal success against perceived failure. Believers who live in relationship with Christ Jesus are certainly not better people. They simply experience the only God who is living and able to give complete forgiveness. Through God's forgiveness they receive the power to know Him and serve Him. Without a relationship with God, they too, would be trapped at the mirror. Only God can take away failure and sin. Only He can offer a fresh new beginning as though no sin had ever touched our life. All those years ago, this is what Jesus wanted the woman at the well to understand. It's what He wants everyone today to understand. Freedom from our failures and our sin is available to all. God positions Himself in order that we might come to know Him. The cross of Jesus Christ is the greatest example we have of God positioning Himself in order that all may be set free. Because He has chosen to enter into the life of those who believe in Him, this positioning empowers them and makes them of service to Him.

---

22 Therefore, no condemnation now exists for those in Christ Jesus. Romans 8:1 HCSB

When God's power to accomplish His will
is acknowledged, the ultimate outcome is
surrendered to His Sovereign will.

As we live in relationship with God, we naturally desire to see His power at work in us. Perhaps you are like me. When you are involved in an area where God is at work, do you envision how things will end up? It is so easy for us to believe that because we see God's work in a specific way and because we sacrificially get involved, we can expect a certain outcome. I have led Bible study groups, taught Sunday school classes, and led church retreats. Countless times as I have prayed and prepared, I have also envisioned the great way God would move during these special gatherings. It seemed natural to me that I could expect, based upon my hours of study and prayer; God would do a great thing.

Once when I led a retreat in the early years of my ministry to women, I excitedly prepared, prayed, and talked with others about this upcoming event. It was one of the first times I had been invited to travel and speak outside my home state. Believing that, finally God had enlarged the area of my ministry, I went to great lengths to be assured that every detail and possibility was considered. I traveled carrying with me a carload of material. Wanting to be prepared for any possible spiritual need that might arise, I'm certain I must have looked like a Bible sales person en route. My traveling companion and I arrived before anyone else. Much to our dismay, we found the retreat site had not been cleaned and prepared. We quickly set about sweeping and preparing our building into a place of worship. As the women arrived, it seemed that their agenda was largely focused on an overnight get-a-way from husbands, children, and jobs. They unloaded a truckload of snacks and headed off to their rooms. We heard no talk or anticipation of what God might do in our midst. In our evening session it seemed like I was cutting into their fun time together. During the night I prayed in preparation for the sessions the following day. In the early morning hours I developed a mild migraine headache and found myself kneeling not in prayer but before the great porcelain throne in the bathroom.

Somehow I got through the morning session and was greeted by a dear lady. I was so excited that she had come to talk to me believing that finally God had moved in someone's heart. She kindly stated how she thought she had gotten the gist of the retreat, and she was headed out for the area garage sales. She exclaimed, "It's pretty hard to pass up a good morning of garage sales!" At the close of the final session of the retreat not a single public decision was made for Christ. No one even came forward to pray. I wasn't sure I had connected with them at all. Feeling exhausted and let down by God, I was ready to crumble in the car for the ride home.

When I returned home that evening, I headed straight for my bathroom to find solace in a warm, soaking bath while trying to understand what had gone wrong. Reclined in the tub, I began to weep and question God. I was new to full-time ministry and I questioned myself, my ministry, even my ability to fulfill what I believed God had led me to do. I didn't understand why, after so many hours of preparation and prayer, God seemed to have deserted me. Almost instantly I sensed His word to me. It was as though God were speaking to me, not audibly of course, but deep within my spirit. I sensed Him saying to me, "This retreat was for you. If you are to go out as I have called you to do, serving Me and representing Me, then it is necessary for you to know of abandonment just as I did."

I learned a powerful lesson that day. The outcome is always His! He may be doing something I am totally unaware of. He knew the hearts of all involved in that retreat, both theirs as well as mine. Out of God's great love and purpose for me, He taught me a valuable lesson through that experience. I saw what it was like for Him when He faced rejection. I also had a new sense of understanding His emotions upon the cross and His feeling of abandonment. Experiencing this truth brought about an intimacy with Him that I have never known in a deeper way. The following morning I went to church and as I entered the worship service, I discovered we would be taking Communion. I wept throughout the observance of the bread and the drink understanding the obedience of my Lord as I never had before. No other table of communion has ever been sweeter to me. There are times when we truly cannot see how God is working. In our obedience we must place our trust in the God who never leaves us. Even when we cannot see how He is working, through our obedience we will see the power of God evidenced in our lives. Obedience does come with sacrifice. Praise God, it also comes with blessing.

> A tragic or unexpected end to ministry does
> not mean that God has finished using us.

Isn't it just like Satan to want us to feel defeated? Who is more qualified to speak about defeat than he? Satan is not a fool; he knows there is no victory that is lasting for him. Any temporary victory he might celebrate must be obtained through luring God's creation to feel defeat alongside him. Because our Lord is a God of awesome power, any feelings of loss, hopelessness, or defeat never come from Him. Still, it is true that He does allow times of despair and loss. God allows these seasons in order that His power may be more evident as He is able to work in and through these experiences. In times when I could not sense God's presence or understand how He was working, it helped me to recognize and claim all that God *is* and Satan *is not.* I realized discrediting Satan would ultimately lead me to a sharper focus on the hope I had in God. With a more refined focus on God, His power became more and more evident to me. My first real understanding of the battle Satan can wage on us came early in my understanding of ministry.

My husband, Ray and I were serving in our first church following Ray's seminary education. He had been called to this church to serve as the Minister of Education and Youth. He was twenty eight years old and I was just twenty three. We were hardly skilled at ministry. My one qualification was that I loved the Lord and wanted to serve Him. This was the only qualification God needed. He started with me as He found me and began to mold the clay of my heart into a vessel for His use. I had, many years earlier quietly told the Lord and publicly told my church that I believed God wanted to use my life in ministry. I had no idea at that time just how that would come about.

Now I found myself married to a minister and serving a group of young people who were eager to know of the things of God and how to give Him leadership of their lives. God brought alongside us other young servants who were skilled both in ministry and knowledge of The Bible. A strong youth ministry was formed and our group grew to about seventy five young people. Nearly two years into our leadership with this group, and after God had continued to grow me in my understanding of His ways and what it was to truly serve Him, a young man quietly entered our youth group during a Wednesday evening gathering.

A high school friend who attended our group had invited David to come with him to church that evening. David was likeable and friendly, yet in so many ways he seemed quite fragile. He was very handsome with dark hair and big brown eyes. Because of his good looks, every girl in the youth group would have sought to date him but he had one characteristic that seemed to prevent this. His effeminate mannerisms and compulsive behaviors regarding his looks kept others at a distance. While most everyone in the group befriended him, girls showed no interest in dating him. He had a sense of humor and laughed often. However, his laugh seemed to mask something he wanted no one else to know or see. He was like a sponge when he listened to the teachings of Christ and almost immediately made the decision to receive the gift of life that belief in Jesus offered. He became very involved in our church and attended everything we offered.

Not long after David joined our group, he entered a prayer meeting one evening visibly shaken and with stark evidence that he had been beaten. We immediately took him to a private place where we could comfort him and discuss what had happened. It was revealed that David lived alone with an alcoholic father. His father had beaten him during a drinking binge. We began the process of contacting Social Services and temporarily placing David in a safe environment. Fortunately, his father acknowledged his need for treatment and immediately went into an in-patient program. We felt that in order for David to remain a part of our body of believers and grow in his new relationship with Christ, he needed to be placed in a foster home that would give him this kind of support. We began to pray about this.

Ray and I soon realized that God was at work in these circumstances in a very personal way in our lives. We had a strong desire to parent and had been unsuccessful in conceiving a child. We had experienced the loss of the baby a year before and had been told by doctors that conception would now be unlikely for us. We had bought a three-bedroom home that seemingly we were unable to fill with children. Now we found ourselves, positioned somewhat as Jesus did, when He met the Samaritan woman at the well. We stood at a *well of ministry* with this young man who needed a home.

After praying about our position and David's need, we made the decision to become certified as foster parents so that he would be allowed to move into our home. This would enable him to remain in the body of believer's he so desperately needed. It was quite an experience to move from having no children to having responsibility for a fifteen year-old boy. I often said we didn't have two a.m. feedings but rather we jumped into having a foster son who simply ate all the time.

About one week into our decision I began to feel we had made a wrong choice. I was, after all, only ten years older than David and really didn't have the role of a typical parent. I often spoke the words, "I can't," rather than the words of Phil. 4:13, "I am able to do all things through Christ who strengthens me." I had no idea when making the decision to become David's foster parent that the abuse, abandonment, and dysfunctional examples that had marked his short life carried with it such deep scars. I simply wasn't prepared for this level of ministry. We learned a great deal about caring for broken lives through our time with David.

It was discovered that his mother had abandoned him at six months of age. He had been shuffled from one relative to another throughout all of his formative years. During his early childhood years he had lived with a dysfunctional relative who resented that he was a boy and had grown his hair shoulder-length and dressed him as a girl. We were shown pictures of this abuse. David's feminine mannerisms began to have meaning to us and we could see that his empty laughter masked a sewer of pain and abuse. Even with this understanding and a heart-felt compassion, we felt very inept at the task before us. This young man could only be described as a broken vessel. The tragic effects of rejection and abuse seemed to seep out of every broken part of his life. Knowing this and also knowing that Christ had entered David's life now brought us to a place of greater understanding as to why Jesus was seated at the well on that day so long ago. Not only did God desire to use us in David's life, but He was also teaching us that He was fully able to equip us for the task. There is no verse to be found that says this is an easy task. It is simply that we are invited to join God as He works in others' lives. And so we accepted this invitation.

David lived with us for nearly a year while his father was in an alcohol treatment program. Throughout the time of treatment he worked with social services to regain custody. Ultimately David returned to his father's home, graduated from high school and moved out on his own. Adulthood brought David temptations he found himself succumbing to. He broke away from the fellowship of other believers and followed a path that seemed to give to him the acceptance he had struggled to find from others. Gay bars and a lifestyle associated with that scene became a part of his life. He felt he had not only found acceptance but also the temporary relationships he seemed to move in and out of gave him brief episodes of feeling he was wanted. Sadly, he was always in great conflict and never seemed to find real peace. Early one Easter morning David chose to end his life while sitting alone in a closed, running car parked inside a garage.

Suicide is always a tragic death. It causes those who have touched the individual's life to feel a gamut of emotions not experienced with other deaths. It is nearly impossible for those left behind to not question how you might have influenced the individual and perhaps helped them to make a different choice. There is always the lingering question of what you might have done or said differently. These questions can be accompanied by a guilty feeling of responsibility for the outcome. Throughout this experience

I found myself confronting many of these issues. I also found it difficult to understand how God's purposes were being fulfilled through something that seemed so tragic and without meaning.

During this time in my life God used this painful situation and loss to lead me to a place of understanding that we are not responsible for the outcome of ministry where we have truly allowed God to use us. I would never have chosen to walk through that time in David's life. Feeling incapable, I would have turned away. As God led us to cross paths with David, we responded to His leadership. Because of that, David was able to come to embrace the love of God. He came to visit me just days before he ended his life. Because of that visit and the conversation we shared, I have complete assurance that David lives for eternity. He is finally in peace today with his Father in Heaven. He did not live in peace here on this earth nor did he die in peace, but I am certain he had accepted the love that only Jesus could give him. Nothing has the power to separate us from that love![23] For a period of time, short-lived as it was, God invited us to give to David a small window of time during which we could exhibit the love of Jesus. It was a love which he had never had in a safe and God-loving environment. The outcome of that ministry was always in God's hands, never in ours. This is as it should be for each of us. In every circumstance where God gives us the opportunity to join His work in someone else's life, He will take responsibility for the outcome. While David's suicide certainly wasn't what God willed for him, God used the outcome in positive ways. David's death was for me, the beginning of accepting the truth that in every situation, I could always trust God regardless of the outcome.

This early lesson at an unfair grave is what sustained me that day so many years later sitting in the car and grieving with a broken heart following my friend Phyllis' death. God may not seem present, and your circumstances may seem to have no purpose. Believe me: dear one, you can trust Him! No matter what, He is present, even when you cannot see it or understand it.[24] On that truth you can depend.[25]

---

23 For I am persuaded that neither death nor life, nor angels nor rulers, nor things present, nor things to come, nor powers, nor height nor depth, nor any other created thing will have the power to separate us from the love of God that is in Christ Jesus our LORD. Romans 8:20 HCSB

24 God is our refuge and strength, a helper who is always found in times of trouble. Psalm 46:1 HCSB

25 We know that all things work together for the good of those who love God; those who are called according to His purpose. Romans 8:28 HCSB

Chapter Four

Pictures of Pain and Suffering

*How to Exhibit a Strong Faith in God Both In Our
Failures and Our Victories*

The ability to prevail and exhibit a strong faith in
God is not found in the character of the individual.
It is found in the source they turn to for their
strength. God alone is our source of strength.

Long before I understood the term handicapped or disabled, the experiences of my childhood gave me front row seats in an arena of pain and suffering. The drama I witnessed in my youth taught me many lessons without any words being spoken. Perhaps this is the reason I am to this day, a visual learner. These lessons remain as visual pictures in my mind, a scrapbook of sorts, revealing a painful time in my life. Although painful, as I reflect back, I realize that this mental scrapbook filled with the memories of my father is really the greatest legacy he has left me.

My father was such a handsome man. His ruddy skin and full dark hair always made me feel he was more handsome than any of my friends' fathers. Daddy loved his hair and carefully cared for it. He gave great attention to both his hair and his shoes. He would polish his shoes with the same delicate care other men exhibited while waxing their automobiles. He felt a man should look groomed from head to toe. (Secretly, we laughed at the clothing matches he would make with colors, stripes, and plaids.) Daddy had an unceasing sense of humor and wit, always taking great pleasure in playing jokes on those he loved. Nothing brought more laughter to him than setting up a good joke and then standing by to enjoy his prey becoming the brunt of his humor. Snickering in the background, I would watch as he and my uncle would scheme together to catch my mom in one of their pranks. Daddy loved when my uncle would show up with a rubber chicken or some other oddity they could use to set up their jokes. They would sit stone-faced and then howl in laughter as she responded to whatever attempt they had succeeded in accomplishing. They were like two playful young boys even in middle age.

Because my father worked for a large hospital as a materials manager, he processed the huge inventory of supplies for patient care. In the preschool years of my life, the mental pictures in my memories are of my dad working. One of the great memories I have in my childhood is when he chose me to go to work with him one Saturday. I helped sweep and clean in the large warehouse, and he ordered hotdogs for lunch. Together we cleared a spot on his desk and shared lunch. I took my job that day quite seriously. After all, I was a wage earner adding a dime to my piggy bank when I returned home. Sometimes we went as a family to his workplace. The building seemed so huge to me and we would have great fun hiding from one another.

Throughout his young adulthood, Daddy experienced symptoms of rheumatoid arthritis. Swollen joints, accompanied with excruciating pain, marked this debilitating autoimmune disease. As he grew older the disease progressed and as a very young child I remember watching my father's body and his gait begin to change. Along with these changes came differences in the touch of his hand. Eventually, we couldn't hold hands in the same way others could. Since his fingers were curled, my small hands would wrap around both his hand and fingers, much like holding a fist. As a child I didn't think of a fist as something gentle, yet he was very much a picture of gentleness to me. Reflecting back now as an adult, I realize that while there was gentleness in his ways and often humor in his personality, I imagine there was pain for him both emotionally and physically.

Alcohol began to become a part of the scrapbook of my memories. As a younger adult, Daddy had enjoyed drinking alcohol. I suppose as the years went by and in his effort to cope with each level of the disease progression, he increased his alcohol consumption. In many ways, I am sure it seemed to him to be a logical escape from both the reality of the disease and the unceasing pain. Both of these now threatened to rob him of his humor, his looks, and his life dreams. The alcohol brought with it not only a change in his ways of fathering but also changes in the environment of our home. My dad was a hard-working, independent man who found he was facing physical challenges he could not control. Though medications were available, they were not what they are today. As medical research and technology have advanced in the last few decades, options are available today that didn't exist in the years he encountered his disease. Great advancements have been achieved in the pharmaceutical field. Multiple anti-inflammatory drugs now readily available over the counter and joint replacement surgeries were unheard of in the days of dad's diagnosis and treatment. Even with the drugs that were available, alcohol anesthetized in a way that gave him an immediate escape and became his drug of choice. Doctor's cautioned dad against the false security of comfort that the alcohol brought, and also the ill effect it had on his body.

Sadly, an entirely different disease, for which little research had been done, was invading Daddy's body. In addition to the swollen joints of his knuckles, hands, knees, and feet, he was now losing muscle mass. My father's body was being invaded by one of the many disorders categorized as muscular dystrophy. He had what is known as Charcot-Marie-Tooth in addition to the rheumatoid arthritis. With this disorder the myelin fibers of his nerves were being destroyed. This resulted in muscle mass loss. Even with the episodes of binge drinking, daddy strived desperately to continue to work, provide for his family, and give every appearance of functioning normally. This would soon change.

My mother, no doubt, had her own set of fears and frustrations. She found herself in her early twenties with five children, an alcoholic husband whose health was slowly deteriorating, and little hope of life improving. In spite of her best efforts to influence him to abandon the alcohol, her words fell upon deaf ears. She was the daughter of an alcoholic father and she knew first-hand what the long-term effect would be. When the stress of her life became overwhelming, she elected to join Daddy in his drinking and together they surrendered to circumstances they couldn't control. It wasn't until my dad's body could no longer handle the mix of alcohol with the disease that we entered a time of crisis.

I have no memories of Daddy going to the hospital or what certainly were recurrent medical appointments. The experience of debilitating disease came at a time when children were not as involved in the sharing of medical information as they are today. It was customary for children to be protected from information as a way of shielding them from the realities that treatments brought about. The uncertain future of Daddy's condition probably wasn't even clear to my mother yet. Withholding information about things like illness, death, and finances was typical and seen as protective of children. Certainly as young as we were, we didn't have the ability to process all that my parents were facing, and so we were shielded from information. In those days we did not have the Internet with its vast resources of easily accessed information. It was a time when the medical doctor was the resource of knowledge regarding health, and the physician's spoken word was rarely questioned. It would have been a rarity in that day for medical news to be shared openly in a family with young children.

How things have changed! When my mother gave birth to my brother, who was the first boy after three girls, she came home from the hospital and I was amazed with what she brought in when she returned. As a four year old, I vaguely remember thinking she had gone to the hospital and picked him out in the same way she went to the grocery store and selected chickens. As a preschooler, I certainly thought he squawked like a chicken! The communication of medical information and the sharing of medical experiences have certainly changed. Who could have imagined there would come a time when entire families, even young children, would fill a delivery room and observe the birth of a child?

Things changed drastically for our family. As the diseases continued to take ownership of my father's body, he had no choice but to surrender to it. The doctor's aided him in making the excruciating decision to file for medical disability. Daddy never went to work again. He would awaken many mornings with swollen knees and unable to walk to the bathroom, I would see him crawl. Over time, Daddy's hands became so atrophied that his fingers curled touching his palms. He wore specially fitted shoes that were much like military boots. His high arches and curled toes made it painful for him to ever be fitted for anything else. Even though the shoes were boot-like, Daddy, ever-mindful of his looks, took great time to keep them polished.

Because these changes in health brought about enormous adjustments both emotionally and financially, my parents still succumbed to binge episodes of escaping with alcohol. When someone is involved in binge drinking they consume large amounts of alcoholic beverage with the primary intention of becoming drunk within a short period of time. My parent's binges would sometimes last for a period of a few days. Then life would return to periods of sobriety. In spite of the binge drinking and all that comes with being the child of an alcoholic, I admired my parents' tenacity, their love, and their commitment. While my album of memories holds many pages I would rather tear away and not reflect on, I realize now that even those times were a part of how God would reveal Himself to me in later years. Growing up in a home of binge alcoholism brought a strange mix of memories. There were absolutely wonderful experiences during times of sobriety, but there were also heart-wrenching times during the episodes of drinking. I didn't realize then just how God was, no doubt, looking on and while bitterly sad at some of the experiences, all the while, He knew that even this He would use for His glory.

Even though Daddy had lost his employment and went on permanent disability, he taught us an invaluable lesson of a strong work ethic. He was a man who was deeply committed to working in whatever ways he could and in spite of his physical limitations, he did just that. As a child I had no understanding of what it must have felt like to be in his position. Having a wife and five young children who looked to him for things he could no longer provide must have been heartbreaking for him. Being a man who had always worked and been self-sufficient to then find himself without that identity had to be excruciating. I imagine there were times when the episodes of binge drinking came in direct response to his emotions as well as his own sense of pride and masculinity.

My family remained active in our church throughout the binge episodes and my album of memories is filled with the wonderful way our church family supported us. There are few memories of their judgment although I imagine most everyone knew of the alcoholism. Instead, I have memories of brightly-colored Thanksgiving baskets of donated food lining the front of our sanctuary. As a child sitting on the church pew with all my siblings beside me, we would gaze at the bushel baskets wrapped in autumn-colored crepe paper and we whispered to one another which tempting basket we hoped would come to our home. Then, just as though God heard our words whispered during the pastor's sermon, the very baskets we longed for would arrive at our door.

Daddy always found ways to generate additional income. He would take us with him to local thrift shops, and we would often drive around to the back of the store. There we would find bicycles that had been cast off as rejects. Daddy became friends with the managers of these shops, and they would sometimes let us have these broken bicycles. I laugh now at this memory. Surely these bicycles must have been in pretty bad shape if even the thrift shop rejected them. We would take them home, replace wheels and chains and then we would help paint them. He would take them to public auctions and sell them. We would celebrate our sale with a tailgate picnic of bologna sandwiches at the local park.

Many years later while at home visiting, I asked Daddy about the emotions of that time in his life. His response is a large part of the legacy he has left me. He shared how hard it was at first to accept changes in his health for which he had no control. During this later time in his life he had overcome the alcohol addictions and had come to a place of peace about the course of his life. He was actively involved in church as a deacon and I had witnessed him going to homes to deliver groceries to widows who were no longer able to go out and make their own purchases. Daddy enjoyed the pleasure of being able to accomplish a task. He didn't allow shame to prevent him from service to others. This was a lesson God allowed me to learn through observing my Dad. I am certain The Lord knew I would need this lesson in my own adulthood. It was an incredible legacy to be able to look at my father's life from my earliest memories and then ultimately see this man, who gave all physical appearances of weakness, now exude such strength.

When we encounter obstacles that seem to rob us of our joy and happiness in life or perhaps alter our dreams and the future we planned, we don't have the ability to see the scope of our circumstance in its entirety. We may pray for God to give us eyes that see things with His perspective. We may ask for hearts that will have understanding and are submissive to His will. Then God bestows a treasure upon us: we find ourselves in the presence of a believer who has learned to persevere in the midst of suffering. It can be a living lesson for us when we see one who struggles and at times even fails in the journey of trusting God. We can learn that through the worst of things, we can prevail with God's help. God's love, compassion, strength, and power are often mirrored for us through the lives of others who have not walked an easy path. The lesson we may learn in this if we are willing to carefully observe, is that the power to prevail and exhibit a strong faith in God is not found in the character of the individual. It is instead found in the source they turn to for their strength. God alone is our source of strength. His strength then in turn develops the character necessary and the faith that prevails no matter what circumstance we face.

My dad taught me many lessons in the process of mirroring to me the power of God in his life. Looking back through my memories, I now realize the privilege of being in this school of instruction. I learned life lessons both in my father's positive responses as well as the destructive and negative reactions to his life. It is easy for one to feel the negative environment in which they may have been exposed to in their childhood has no purpose or value. Certainly in cases of abuse or neglect where one has been the recipient of inflicted pain, one does not find purpose or attribute this to God's will. Circumstances such as this are never His will. The lessons I am speaking of are those learned by observing how other believers allow God to show His strength and power both when they succeed and also when they fail.

Looking back on my childhood and the journey into adulthood, I now place great value on having been able to observe my father both fail and succeed. Having these experiences with my earthly father has brought insight into my relationship with my Heavenly Father. The insights I have gained have produced what I call "Solid Rocks of Truth" that are foundational to my faith. They form in my mind, the picture I have of God. Perhaps in sharing them you too will use these rocks of truth to build for yourself a mental picture of God. They help to visually establish the character of our God while recognizing that His character is not dependent upon ours. These rocks of truth about Him do not change in response to the way we respond to Him.

Solid Rocks of Truth

God's love is not based upon our choices.

First and foremost in the lessons I learned, is the fact that the presence of God's great love does not depend on my choices. He did not give up on my dad. Even when Daddy made choices that certainly didn't please God, I saw great examples of The Lord watching over us, providing for us, and just responding in the way any loving parent would do. This is how I was able to see God as a loving and caring Father. The Lord never withdrew love no matter how vile the appearance of sin seemed to be. I learned from an early age that I would always have God's great love to reach out to no matter how ugly or unlovable the sin of my life appeared. It is a truth that even today I often rely upon. I know in the midst of some of the choices I make there are times I certainly must appear unlovable. Still, I am assured that even in the worst of my sin I am never unlovable to Him. This truth can be yours if you will believe it is available and receive it. Friend, do not be afraid to reach out to God and experience the kind of love you can receive from no other source. It is available to you no matter how vile the appearance of your sin may be.

Repentance of sin is never motivated by the judgment of others who are observing while someone fails.

I learned of repentance watching my parents. I remember times as a young child that I watched from a distance as my parents would kneel together and ask God for forgiveness. We can be enamored with dramatic testimonies offered in church services proclaiming wondrous events God has performed in individuals' lives. This is rightly so, as our God is an awesome and powerful God who never enters into a life without changing it. It honors God to praise Him for this. As I grew up attending church, it allowed me the opportunity to hear such testimonies. I learned how God could change a life. I noticed, however, there were few testimonies that alluded to the continued struggle of failing after repentance. When a believer is somewhat of a repeat offender in an area of sin, they may feel they shouldn't tell this part of their testimony. In spite of God's forgiveness, they may have returned to their sin more than once in their journey of trusting God completely. Because we love a happy ending, we are somewhat conditioned to respond better when we hear a testimony ending with complete success. We are able to celebrate the good work of our Lord and not be confronted with the reality of further temptations or sins. I learned through my dad's life that the testimony doesn't end with our redemption. It is, of course, the highlight of our life's story, but every day we live, both in struggle and victory, we are a living testimony still being written by the hand of God. God uses our struggles and even our failures for His good work. A scowl of judgment or condemnation never motivated me to reach out for the love of God. True repentance for doing wrong is always motivated by love. This solid rock of truth brings into focus a consistent picture of God as love. The Bible tells us God *is* love.[26]

> The testimony God is writing with our lives is being
> written to demonstrate His character not ours.

When God shows Himself to be strong and when He gently loves us in our struggles and failures, He is writing a testimony of His character not ours. Our response to God in the midst of difficult circumstances or the poor choices we make is pivotal in God using our lives as tools of instruction for someone else. Our prayers should not be for *us* to have the strength to turn from our sin. None of us has this strength within ourselves. This is why John, the beloved disciple, wrote Jesus' words to us.

---

26 And we have come to know and to believe the love God has for us. God is love, and the one who remains in love remains in God, and God remains in him. I John 4:16 HCSB

"I am the vine; you are the branches, the one who remains in Me, and I in him produce's much fruit; because you can do nothing without Me."[27] Where does the power lie? It is in God and not within us. What a gift this is to us. It sets us free from feelings of hopelessness in overcoming areas of sin that seem to hold us in bondage. All of us have areas of repeated temptation and sin. We may often feel defeat to the degree that we resist even talking with God about it again. Satan loves for us to be in this position, but it is never one God intended us to have. This solid rock of truth in my mental picture of my God causes me to know that in spite of my failure in certain areas of repeated sin, God wants to hear from me. He wants me to surrender in that battle and give Him the chance to show me His great power. While I may have failed at times, He has led me to victory in *His* strength and *His* character which is unfailing. Areas of sin that I never thought I would conquer have become less and less of a battle as I have learned to call out to Him in prayer.

God will ultimately be glorified as Christians live out both failures and victories through God's strength and character. Our life lived before mankind teaches them that our God is not only the source of our faith, but He is also the perfecter of it.[28] The great power of the hope given to us in Christ is manifest as we fix our eyes on Jesus in the midst of all we endure.

Jesus did this for us when He set His eyes on pleasing the Father and fulfilling His purpose. He looked beyond the shame and suffering of the cross, and He set His eyes on the joy that lay before Him.[29] You may ask what joy he possibly considered in the midst of his own crucifixion. The joy He would have felt my friend, is you! The joy Christ went to the cross to obtain was the delight of making it possible for you to enter into a personal relationship with Him. It was the treasure of knowing the power this would bring into your life.

God's power is never limited by our
feelings of hopelessness.

---

27 "I am the vine; you are the branches. The one who remains in Me and I in him produces much fruit, because you can do nothing without Me." John 15:5 HCSB

28 ...Keeping our eyes on Jesus, the source and perfecter of our faith, who for the joy that lay before Him endured a cross and despised the shame, and has sat down at the right hand of God's throne. Hebrews 12:2 HCSB

29 Hebrews 12:2 HCSB

For those who had chosen to follow Jesus, the day of Christ's crucifixion was a picture of hopelessness. They no doubt believed that their relationship had come to an end on the day of His death and burial. That may be how it outwardly appeared to them, but God was at work. How many times in the midst of our circumstances do we feel a loss of hope? We all encounter times we feel as those disciples did. We may succumb to despair and believe it is the end. When there is a broken marriage or financial crisis, a wayward child, or other similar crisis, we may succumb to despair and believe it is the end. How do we find joy in such a time as we live today? Temptations from Satan seem to have never been greater upon mankind. The massive effect of drugs and alcohol, along with the increase of its destructive outcomes are the result of the countless lures Satan has cast out upon our world. He is unleashing his power because he knows he is not a part of the last act of God's story. Just as it wasn't the end for those precious believers who huddled together following Jesus' burial, the apparent hopelessness of our circumstance is not the end. Those disciples surely felt devastated and even fearful. Just like them, we too haven't seen the last act of our Lord. Believe it my friend, God is alive and He is still working in our midst. You may not have read His entire book, The Bible, but take a peek at the end. God wins! Don't you want to be on His side?

With Jesus' burial, God had not finished His work. While those who loved Him and followed Him probably sat together sharing stories and comparing memories, I imagine they spoke as though it had ended. Jesus lay lifelessly in a cold stone grave, and everything about that reality had to evoke feelings of hopelessness for His followers. It may have appeared that way but it was anything but the end. Jesus had faced death knowing He would be raised to life. While hopelessness seemed to engulf His followers, that grave did not remain silent. This teaches a great truth to us. No matter how things may appear, God is still working.

God raised Jesus out of that grave and now He sits beside the Father with His ear turned to your prayer and His voice calling out your name.[30] This is a picture I absolutely love to envision. He calls out my name and my need to Father God. He speaks of His great love for me, as every resource of Heaven is unleashed on my behalf. I may consider every reason why He might not respond. He on the other hand considers all that *He* is and all *He* has to offer. In His great love, He responds.

---

30 Therefore He is always able to save those who come to God through Him, since He always lives to intercede for them. Hebrews 7:25 HCSB

The resources of God are limitless.

What are these resources, you may ask? In my search to know my Lord in a greater way and with a deeper understanding of who He is, I discovered many attributes He would bring into my life. Some of these qualities I had long ago discovered about God. Still, I didn't realize then that as a part of the relationship with Him, He would fully bring me to experience these qualities more personally. I began to learn what power is available to me in this relationship. I discovered that I didn't have to appear a certain way or strive to mirror Him. Instead, He bestowed His hope, His joy, His knowledge, etc. As you grow in your relationship with God, you will discover that the list could go on and on. In an effort to help you search the scriptures and begin to discover for yourself how great the gift of your salvation is, I have given you a guide at the end of this chapter. I pray that through it you will often be reminded of all that is yours in Christ.

When you or a fellow believer struggles with an area of sin, turn your eyes away from the sin. Turn to the awesome, powerful God who redeems us. Call upon Him to rescue in His great love and then begin to celebrate the glory God will receive as your prayers are answered. Practice celebrating the power of God even before evidence of your victory is apparent. As you turn your focus from the sin and turn to the solid rocks of truth that you know about your God you will begin to grow in a deeper relationship with Him. You will see victories not only for your life but also for those whom you love and pray for. Not only will you become a powerful intercessor for a brother or sister in Christ, but also you protect yourself from being caught in Satan's lure to either judge them or feel hopeless about their situation. The more you turn to God on their behalf, the more you will mirror his love for them. Repentance, forgiveness, and ultimately fulfilling God's purposes will never come about in someone's life through your judgment.

I know now this was the source of my dad's ability to accept the path his life took with all its physical limitations and the loss of his dreams. Daddy relied on God at times in which I would have felt hopeless. His ability to trust God developed out of God's great love and also the love, acceptance, and prayers of other believers. Was it always a journey marked by constant victory? Certainly it was not. Yet the greatest legacy he gave me is the picture of peace he had when he aligned his life with God's purposes. While he expressed how hard it had been to accept his physical limitations and the loss of his dreams, he was so thankful that God had allowed this to be the course of his life. He acknowledged that he knew he would have been a man of pride and that God had used his limitations to bring him to a place of dependence upon Him. Had it not been for his disabilities, he truly felt that his pride would have kept him from having the relationship with God he had grown to enjoy. Because of that, I heard my father give God thanks for something others would have cursed. Even with the memories of some poor choices along the way, I was so blessed to have this example lived out before me. Sitting at that table with him that day as I questioned him about his life, I heard my Dad give thanks to God for the life He had been given. I didn't realize then that this same prayer would be one I would learn to pray as I faced changes in my own life.

In Christ I Have

A   Access to the Father – Ephesians 2:18
B   Benefits and Blessings – Psalm 116:12
C   Confidence – I John 5:14-15
D   Delight – Psalm 37:4
E   Eternal Life – Romans 6:23
F   Forgiveness – Ephesians 1:7
G   Grace – Romans 5:17
H   Hope – Psalm 119:49
I   Insight –Ephesians 1:8
J   Joy – John 15:11
K   Knowledge – Colossians 2:3
L   Love – John 17:23, John 15:9
M   Mercy – Ephesians 2:4
N   Newness of Life – Romans 6:4
O   Opportunity – Luke 21:13
P   Purpose – I Peter 2:9
Q   Quietness – Psalm 23:2
R   Rest – Matthew 11:28
S   Self Control – I Timothy 1:7
T   Truth – John 14:7, John 16:13
U   Unfading Crown of Glory – I Peter 5:4
V   Victory – Psalm 119:165
W   Wisdom – Psalm 119:99-100
Y   Yoke of Christ – Matthew 11:29
Z   Zeal – Psalm 119:139

Chapter Five

Positioned for God's Power

When Crushing Circumstances or Words Alter our Lives

> God will use the events and circumstances of our lives
> as opportunities for us to participate with Him. He
> uses these times to reveal His willingness to sustain
> us and to give present day revelations of His power.

Throughout the scriptures we can find countless examples of people caught in difficult situations in which they might have doubted God's presence or questioned the way in which God might be working. Some faced dreadful diseases, others imprisonment, and still others the loss of one they loved. While these accounts were lived out many years ago, time doesn't change the reality that our lives are not always filled with joy. Certainly some of the same difficulties we read of in The Bible are experiences we sometimes face today. We too face disease, loss and heartbreak. In these ways their lives were much like ours. We look to the scriptures for guidance and wisdom in how to confront our own difficulties. How often do we face an event with an attitude that seeks to discover how God might be present and allowing us the opportunity to be a current day revelation of His love and power? This does not easily become an automatic response for us. We must seek to develop thoughts that consider how God may be at work in whatever we find ourselves confronting.

Because we are human flesh, we are easily drawn to thoughts of how our circumstance affects us personally. We may not begin to seek out God's involvement until we have already considered our own personal options. Perhaps this is why many come to a place of seeking God only when they are at the end of themselves. When they feel they have exhausted all means of handling a situation they may then turn to God through the scriptures or the counsel of another believer. Don't you just wonder how God might be able to reveal Himself to us if we trained our responses to acknowledge Him from the beginning of an event in our life? How might we come to know God in a more personal way if this were our immediate response? How might others come to know God more vividly as they observed our response?

> God may lead us into circumstances in which we may
> not initially see the way He is present and working.

Let me share with you an example of how God was not initially recognized in an event of my life. During my late twenties I began to experience changes in the structure of my hands. Gradually my fingers and the bones of my hands appeared bent and somewhat twisted. It became a struggle to grasp things. This change was followed by pain and muscle weakness in my lower extremities. Slowly, but still evident over the next decade, I had undeniably loss muscle mass in both my hands and my feet. The loss had occurred so gradually over time, and initially, denial was easy. Few people outside of those closest to me even recognized that there were any changes. Then along with the muscle loss, pain became a daily companion. By my late thirties I could no longer mask physical changes with casual excuses and serious denial.

While I knew intellectually the facts that I saw playing out in my physical health, I also knew there was no cure for Charcot-Marie-Tooth, (CMT), the same disorder of muscular dystrophy my father had lived with. Because my father also lived with the crippling disease of rheumatoid arthritis, I had memories tucked far away in my mind of the experiences my father had endured and I couldn't imagine living that out with my own children. There had been times during my childhood I would watch as my father struggled to do things other dads could easily do with their children. I had seen him stumble and sometimes fall in public places. I had even observed people, who didn't understand, laugh from the sidelines as he struggled to get up.

During my adolescence and well into my early teen years I felt embarrassment when my friends would see my dad fall. I didn't have the maturity or the ability to explain to my friends why my dad was different than theirs. Just as medical technology, information and family involvement in health have increased, so has understanding and sensitivity to people with disabilities. In the time my father struggled with his loss of health, the *Americans with Disabilities Act*, created to protect the rights of the disabled, did not exist. There were no handicapped license plates, preferred parking spaces, or educational resources for public awareness. As difficult as it is for me to admit, there were times during my adolescence and teen years that I felt embarrassment about my father's appearance. When I found myself facing some of the same disabilities, I could hardly bear the thought of those past experiences and the feelings I imagined my own children might endure.

Because others in my extended family had been diagnosed with CMT, I knew the process one went through in order to be tested and ultimately diagnosed. I knew this testing process could be painful and I reasoned that if there were no cure, then why would it be practical to go through the testing? Layers of denial grew deeper and deeper as I watched myself deteriorate in muscle strength and grow more in pain with each passing year. Finally in my forties, I found myself unable to deny the many changes I felt happening to my body. Although my three children were now in their early teens and while I feared the effects that having a disabled mother would have on them, I was forced to seek medical attention.

Ironically, I was employed at a hospital just as my father had been all those years ago. With the passing of time, I had begun to easily injure my ankles and feet. I always made excuses for it. I called it "Clumsiness," "Accident-prone" and a host of other titles that would mask the truth that I had a loss of muscle mass. It was an undeniable reality that I could no longer do things I once enjoyed doing. One day while at work, I was walking through my office when suddenly I felt something that seemed to pop in my foot. I immediately sat down and saw that my foot swelling. I was not involved in anything strenuous - simply walking - and yet I had injured myself. I wasn't wearing shoes with high heels and I hadn't twisted or turned my ankle. *I was simply walking.* I had no choice but to leave work and seek medical advice.

This began the process of peeling back layer after layer of denial that I had so successfully built up over the previous two decades. Seeing a podiatrist, an orthopedic surgeon and ultimately a neurologist, I found myself enduring a painful testing procedure. Electromyography, (EMG), is a technique for evaluating and recording the electrical activity produced by skeletal muscles. This test was done along with a Nerve Conduction Velocity Study. Electrodes are placed on the skin over the nerve to be studied. In my case, the nerves of my entire body were studied. An electrical stimulator is placed on the skin near the electrodes and is used to create an electrical current strong enough to fully stimulate the nerve. While the current is no comparison to that of your home's electrical current, it was extremely painful. In CMT patients there is a loss of the myelin fiber which lines all the nerves in our bodies. This fiber is much like an insulator protecting the nerve. Without the myelin fiber the nerve will be destroyed. As the nerve is destroyed muscles no longer receive the stimuli needed and they deteriorate in their function. This is what had happened in my body.

> When crushing events or words are spoken that
> alter our lives, God is at the heart of all we may
> feel emotionally or experience physically.

The diagnosis was exactly as I had expected it would be. Finally the undeniable words were spoken to me; "You have CMT". The neurologist explained that it was a slow, progressive disease and I could expect to gradually lose muscle mass in my arms and legs. Few of the neurologist words really registered in my thoughts. I was exhausted from the testing process as well as the stress of knowing I was finally at the place I had fought so desperately to avoid. After a short consultation and discussion of my plan of treatment, I began the physical therapy and a treatment plan that brought about tremendous changes for me.

In so many ways I still did not want to embrace the truth of my diagnosis. I felt there had to be some way I could still control the outcome. Because I was determined to be in control and not allow this to alter my life, physical therapy was scheduled at the hospital where I worked. My plan at that point was to go to work, check in for physical therapy on my break time and proceed with life as normal. Little did I realize that what awaited me just around the corner would to be defined as *anything but* normal?

In the course of physical therapy many assessments were done to measure the loss of muscle mass and the lack of strength and resistance. These measurements allowed the therapist to determine that the progression of the disease was far worse than originally thought. I suffered a much worse foot drop than even I realized. This was a dominant factor in the cause for my falls. A prosthetic device would need to be made for my feet to have support and prevent me from further injury. I had known other people who wore devices inside their shoes and had found relief from other conditions. I assumed that I too would have a similar device to slide into my shoe and correct my problem. Plaster molds were made of my feet and legs. I really didn't understand or perhaps I didn't allow myself to hear and take in the extent of what they were doing. I went to their office to receive what would ultimately change my life.

My husband was out of state attending a conference at the time of my appointment to receive the prosthetics. I had taken the day off from work and arranged for my best friend to go with me. It seemed like the perfect opportunity for us to shop and have lunch following my appointment. Little did I know how this one morning would ultimately become known to me as the time God positioned me to become an instrument of His power. Since then, I have come to realize that our moments of despair are often the times when God is working and His purposes are being accomplished. The process of God at work is often unseen and most often not understood by us. Unless we build a deep trusting relationship with our Lord in the daily journey with Him, we will find ourselves unable to believe in His presence during the experiences that can shake our faith. Without that trust, we will find ourselves unable to believe that He is working. Our most challenging moments can become the greatest times of trusting and experiencing God.

I suppose denial is like a thick blanket that is sometimes hard to toss back. I had in my mind that I would have the therapist slip the little device into my shoe and away I would go to have lunch and shop. I had been told to bring in a pair of gym shoes that laced up. I gave no real thought to this requirement. I thought perhaps women were asked to bring gym shoes as a precaution from entering with high heels that would make the work of the therapist more difficult. As I sat in the examination room, I began to consider the area of town we were in and what shopping would be available to us when we left.

Suddenly an attendant entered with a large set of orthotic braces, carrying one in each hand. They measured approximately fifteen inches tall with metal brackets at each ankle and an attached plastic insert that went under the foot. I had never seen anything like them before. They looked like something a person who was crippled might be seen wearing. I smiled, greeting him as I kindly stated, "Oh those aren't mine; you must have the wrong room." He hesitated and with a confused look, stated that he would be with me momentarily and exited. I continued to read a magazine as I waited. He returned bringing with him another gentleman. His associate was now carrying the large set of orthopedic braces with bolts glistening. They sat down and together they explained to me that these awkward looking devices were in fact mine. With this devastating news he drew another breath and spoke life-altering words. I would be wearing them for the rest of my life.

> The unchanging God remains steadfast even when
> we feel that all of life has been altered. He will use
> other believers to be His comfort, His guidance
> and His encouragement for us to trust Him.

Together they proceeded to tell me it would take some time of adjustment but I would adapt to them. From that point on, all their words droned into somewhat of a hum. They spoke matter-of-factly while I felt the final layer of my denial being torn away. They helped strap the devices into the gym shoes I had brought with me. They peeled back the three-inch blue Velcro straps as they explained how the gym shoes would be the type of shoe I would forever wear now. As they pulled them around the calves of my legs, I sat quiet and motionless. I couldn't imagine that I would *ever* adapt to this.

My mind was racing with all kinds of questions. How can I wear this every day? What would my husband and children think of this? I didn't want to be seen at work this way. What would they think? How would others react to me? Already considering the fashion impact this would have on me as a woman, I thought; "Surely they had different colors of *Velcro* straps. Blue would not match everything I would wear." Can you imagine that in the midst of such a moment, I was giving thought to fashion? My appointment was during the month of August and the heat and humidity were unbearable. How would I learn to tolerate having all this strapped to my legs? Living near the ocean, I even considered how I wouldn't be able to wear these to the beach. My mind raced with so many thoughts and yet

I sat quietly, hardly moving as the two gentlemen celebrated their success in the fitting of these braces.

My racing thoughts were abruptly interrupted as they led me to another room. It was here they would observe me walking in my new devices. I will never forget entering this area. It was a large open room lined with mirrors on every wall. There were bars attached to the wall and oddly to me, it gave every appearance of a dance studio. I had not grown up in a home where dance lessons could be made available; however I had been like many girls who danced as ballerinas in their imaginative play. I, just like many other girls, had pictured myself with beautiful garments flowing; toes pointed and pirouettes of excellence. This now was far from any whimsical dreams I had ever envisioned. I could hardly take in the reflection staring back in every direction. As they directed me, I took hold of the bar and began to walk alongside it. I felt as though I were mountain climbing with some sort of obtrusive leg gear. Little did I realize as I exited the office, just how difficult it would be to face the emotional and mental mountains I would need to climb from that day forward.

The day was spent with my friend but it was far from what we had originally thought it would be. I was trying desperately to be positive while not displaying the collision of emotions I felt inside. I had learned in my childhood to deal with things privately. That day everything I had learned about God was being called upon from deep within my heart. My best friend, Butch sought desperately to not react. She had great training in this herself. Butch was a nickname given to her in her childhood. Hers had not been an easy life and along the way she had developed a deep faith. She had experienced much in her life. She had married a veteran of the Vietnam War. He had served our country during his younger years and had returned home as an amputee. She was very adept at knowing how to comfort and how to encourage. More importantly, she had the skill of doing so with few words. Oh the love of God exhibited to us when He places in our path other servants of His. What a blessing it is to us to have these fellow believers come gently alongside us bringing with them our Lords words. They are His arms and His comfort when we so desperately need this.

With both my husband and my children away, we returned to her home that evening. She busily prepared dinner for us, directing me to take a break and sit with her husband, Mike. She knew he understood what I had no words for. Mike was a strong, masculine mechanic. He would never be described as a soft, coddling individual. He was a man with a strong work ethic who had no patience for individuals who made excuses for laziness. Because of his own injuries and the life he had built for himself in spite of this, he had no tolerance for those who might wallow in their disabilities. Mike talked little about his own disability and had a strong belief that it was not an excuse for an unproductive life. As a mechanic he could build and repair most anything. His hands were often dark from grease as he shuffled through the enormous amount of tools that were his toys. I learned over the years of our friendship that this strong, coarse man who was often engulfed in steel while he worked was really a large hearted caring soul. His demeanor was everything I needed that evening. Mike's advice to me called deep within my soul to draw from a place he could understand like no other person on that evening.

Mike sat before me as a strong example of one who had endured much and yet had come to know the depths of God's riches. He knew the losses that I would yet feel and embrace. However, in no way did he try to prepare the way for that part of the journey. Unlike the men in the prosthetic office, Mike didn't offer a plan or describe what I would yet face or seek to avoid. He simply sat back, sipped his tea and shared only *that* moment alongside me. Throughout that evening he helped me to see how the day's events were just a part of a larger journey. Significant and painful as that day was, I could see in him a hope I didn't have within myself. I wasn't in a position on that evening to believe there would be other days, ones in which I wouldn't feel the sting that this day had brought with it.

Because it was August we sat outside on the deck. Perched upon our seats, together we were quite a pair. He reclined in his shorts having his prosthetic leg fully exposed while I sat propping up my two plastic- encased legs. Somehow I didn't feel as strange in his company that evening. He seemed to know this as well. It was a great example of our loving God who brings us alongside those who know how to be used by Him.

This day became another turning point for me in my journey of truly knowing my God. It would later be seen as the greatest example set before me of the way one can be God's instrument in the life of another. Though I had been a believer for many years, I truly didn't know how to be this kind of instrument. One thing was certain, this couple had learned how to be used by God and I wanted to learn from their example. It became for me, the challenge of living out my faith no matter the circumstances. Could I really realize the great battle that lay ahead? Certainly not! This one thing was clear to me, God had brought along-side me two precious people of faith to aide me in my journey. How this must please our Lord when He observes His children caring for one another. Truly He knew the path he had me traveling. It was his delight to involve others in the journey. I think this always is His desire. I sat with legs bound, emotions shaken and a life riveted by change that would lie ahead. What love God had for me. I couldn't necessarily feel it that day, but I sure saw it through these servants of His.

Chapter Six

※

Unrelenting Faith

Fighting the Temptation to Give Up

God is always working to increase our faith as we journey
through life with Him.
Fear is never God's method of building our faith.

Who facing diminished health doesn't consider the possibility of being healed? Certainly this is why there are so many pathways of pursuing recovery. Consider the patient who is fighting the demise of their health that now threatens to rob them of their dreams, goals, or even their very life. Healing, no doubt, becomes their passionate pursuit, and certainly this pursuit becomes the very air of hope they breathe in order to continue on.

The presence of disease or affliction of any sort naturally leads one to pursue healing. For some, this pursuit becomes the desperate search and battleground for survival. For others, the idea of healing may become a wishful fantasy; something they may not truly dream possible when they are told, "there is no cure."

When a patient is first diagnosed with a debilitating disease they have usually already ridden a roller coaster of emotions leading up to that diagnosis. Prior to exams, testing, consultations, and treatment plans, they have usually exhausted an array of emotional ups and downs. There may have been a time of symptoms or unusual bodily functions indicating a loss of good health. These changes can be frightening, and are often met with denial. The fear that our body is no longer responding in normal ways can trigger a defense within us to deny what we feel or see. This denial becomes our effort to remain in control.

It can be frightening, as it was for me, to realize that your body is diminishing in its ability to function. Regardless of all you do to counter the attack of disease, you struggle when you cannot change what you see and feel happening. It is a powerless position to be in. This fear can be fueled with the enormous amount of information you hear and read about. The flame of fear can also be fanned by information or experiences you have already stored in the database of your mind. This fear erupts from the array of health crisis you have heard about or witnessed in others. Even when you are not facing the same diagnosis as others you have known personally, your imagination may begin to haunt you with a variety of outcomes for yourself. Some of these outcomes are not based upon fact, but rather they are fears or attitudes that have been formed throughout your life experience or the experiences that others have shared with you.

Interestingly, others will share stories with you purely out of a desire to tell you just how bad it was for someone else. Perhaps they intend to help you to see that your circumstance could be worse. These stories, however, only plant fear. Let me encourage you to limit the stories you tell someone who is facing a diagnosis that is life-changing. Their story alone is overwhelming and truly they haven't the room in their thoughts for a story that doesn't bring them hope. To the one facing these fears, let me say that God is never the author of these fears, but He will meet you in them and guide you through the emotional storms they create. While He meets us in our fears, He is never instigating fear as a method for building up our faith.

During the first year of my own diagnosis with CMT, I came face to face with a host of attitudes I had stored deep within myself. My mind became a mental battlefield and both my thoughts and the opinions of others engaged an assault upon my mind. Many of these thoughts were formed out of my own life experience of living with a handicapped father. I confronted an array of assailing darts that erupted out of my own emotions. During the first year after my diagnosis I wasn't certain I would win this battle within myself. Now having the advantage of reflecting back on that time, I realize that my enemy wasn't necessarily the disease, as much as it was my own self.

God offers hope in all circumstances. The body
of Christ should mirror the hope of God with
the same compassion that Christ did.

I can't say I faced my disease with any hope of healing. Even knowing that my condition was one that would deteriorate over time, I was grateful for the knowledge that this type of disorder was a slow-progressing disorder. I was not facing a terminal diagnosis like others I knew. I had friends living with different diseases that brought about the possibility of much more serious outcomes. The reality that I wasn't facing a terminal condition certainly brought relief still, I was furious when well-meaning friends would comment to me, "at least you don't have cancer." Even understanding their intent, may I suggest that you weigh your words carefully as you seek to encourage someone who is freshly encountering a diagnosis of any kind? Most often you will find they do not really need or desire your sympathy, or your attempts to speak words that try to lessen the depth of their pain. While the intent of these words is so often meant for their good, the truth of their diagnosis is fresh and new to them. Your response to it may be interpreted as a careless attitude in the face of what, to them, is an insurmountable reality. What the person most often desires is just empathy.

My greatest encouragers were those who spoke few words but embraced me and allowed me to mourn my loss of health. I was adapting to the reality of leg braces that would now bind my legs from the knees down and I was discarding any shoes that would ever again seem stylish or pretty. During this time I didn't find advice or opinions to be comforting. It offered little help when someone who stood before me in beautiful shoes would voice to me how my braces "Didn't look bad and that with time I would get used to it." Although the intent of statements like this was meant for encouragement it instead made me feel that my pain was being trivialized.

True comfort came from the friend who cried with me as I stood before her for the first time clothed in my new look. As I stood crying and whispering, "Its worse than we thought it would be", she simply embraced me, and said, "I know it is". She didn't offer to me words that were an attempt to diminish the pain or the embarrassment I felt at the way I looked. She had no idea of the tremendous weight of pain-filled memories I carried from watching the life my father had lived. She couldn't know the oppressive fear I had welling up within my thoughts, nor could she comprehend the emotions I was battling at the prospect of how my children may change in their responses to me. In the same way that there had been times as a teenager I had felt embarrassment at my father's image, I now wondered if my own children might feel some of those same emotions about me. The possibility of that brought great sadness to me.

I encourage you to recognize that there are so many more emotions and thoughts than what you perceive someone is facing as they adjust to a diagnosis. These thoughts encompass so much more than just what is visual to you. Limiting your words and increasing your compassion can often be the best formula for meeting the needs of hurting people. God offers hope in all circumstances. The body of Christ should mirror the hope of God with the same compassion that Christ did.

My greatest comforters were those who showed compassion and acknowledged the losses and the pain associated with all that the disease had brought with it. These friends allowed me the freedom to cry, and to openly express my anger and my fear. They ultimately stood with me until I could once again feel joy and hope for my future. It was a huge commitment on their part. It was one that took time and as they allowed that time to pass they didn't offer excessive words or advice. They allowed me to express my attitudes, and work through the process of both my diagnosis, and the progression of my disease. They did not diminish my emotions or the expression of them. They also did not judge me or offer sermons to me when my emotions erupted into expressions of doubts about God, His will, or His love. As these friends who were true sisters in Christ stood by me, and didn't tire of my process, they built a trust with me. Ultimately I arrived at a place of allowing them to express words I needed to hear, however, coming to this place took time. While it may not be the same for everyone confronting a disease or life changes, for me it was through those friends who offered less preaching and greater patience that I most often found hope and peace.

God is more concerned with the process of building our
faith than with the amount of time this process takes.

We live in such a world of speed. We have somewhat developed an obsession for swiftness and lives lived at a rapid pace. We now drive through businesses for most of the services we seek. This eliminates the need to park, wait, or truly interact with people. We drive through, purchase and eat our food while traveling to our next destination. We talk by cell phone

- driving while multi-tasking. We drink, write, and even shave or apply make-up as we move about town. We bank, do our dry cleaning, and wash our car without ever leaving the driver's seat. It is as if unknowingly we are each competing in some sort of reality game in which the prize will be given to the one who achieves the most and gets there the fastest.

When we encounter circumstances that can be life-altering, it becomes nearly unbearable for others around us to allow us the one thing we need, which is time. Because of the way we live as well as the desire to once again see us have joy and hope; well-meaning people may pressure us to move on. It isn't that they intend to do the wrong thing. In fact, they often respond this way because they really do believe they are helping. Even people who love us the most sometimes lack the knowledge of what is the right thing to say or do. As in all of life, Jesus is our model for the kind of compassion we need. He was patient, understanding and slow to speak.

For years I had fought so desperately to cling to my denial. When I could no longer use excuses, then I had to face the hard, cold reality, of not just understanding the term "Handicapped", but of living the life of a disabled person. Adapting to all the emotions I was encountering through these times brought with it a tremendous amount of adjustments for my family as well. Let me encourage you to recognize that when someone in a family encounters the onset of a disease, the entire family is a part of this diagnosis. Shelter the family as a unit in your love, support and care. As I felt that my family was cared for and secure in their emotions, I was better able to focus on my own need to find peace and comfort.

Through the years the Bible had become for me a place of comfort and communication with my God, and so I turned to that source as I sought to understand His thoughts about healing. I had by now experienced the loss of my dad, as well as other dear friends for whom I had prayed for God to heal. As I entered my own encounter of disease, I didn't feel that I had ever witnessed a dramatic earthly healing. Certainly I had never seen any healing such as those I read about in my Bible. This is not to say that there had been none, rather it is just that I had not personally witnessed this.

I had embraced a belief that God was love and I had added to that belief that He was unchanging. I truly believed my Lord was the same powerful God today that I read about in the Bible. Certainly many of the accounts of the Bible were different than His work in our world today. We live in a different age with a completely different culture and way of life. Yet, I believed God was still active in His world, and moved about us in some pretty awesome and powerful ways. I did not so much seek healing for myself as I sought to embrace the presence of God in my situation.

Not only was I exploring more and more about God as a healer for my own understanding, I was at this same time deeply involved in the diagnosis of the malignancy that threatened the life of my dear friend, Phyllis. I was a member of a circle of prayer that was so much deeper than anything I had ever experienced. I sought healing for Phyllis and truly believed that God could heal her, yet I did not have the faith to believe God could do something as dramatic as healing the lame person I had become. If I had embraced the belief that He was an unchanging God who held the same power today that I read about in scripture, I needed to understand what it was that seemed to block my belief that He could do this for me.

As several years passed, I became more and more aware that my muscle weakness was growing worse. In contrast, my relationship with God grew stronger. I began to experience a deeper intimacy with Him in my times of both prayer and Bible study. I continued to seek medical care and advice, but did not want to attempt any surgical procedures that would permanently alter tendons or muscle function. I certainly wanted to delay these procedures as long as I could.

Nearly five years after my diagnosis I began to realize that I would not be able to deny the need for further intervention very much longer. Pain had grown to be a daily part of my life. This pain now involved areas other than my legs and feet. I was experiencing an intense pain in my shoulder that seemed to be unrelated to the CMT. After seeking out medical advice to no avail, I was finally recommended to a pain management doctor. I received cortisone shots and tried some new medications. I had already gone through another EMG test and what became a seemingly endless ritual of physical therapy. I was going through a tremendous amount of daily pain while working full time, being a wife and a mother to teen-age children. All the while I continued to be involved in the ministry of my church. I slowly felt myself breaking down from within. I sat in the doctor's office crying as I lamented, "I don't want to manage the pain, I want to get rid of it!" I entered a time of depression. Those who live with daily pain know exactly what I am saying.

During this time I began to write my prayers in my journal. It was such a lonely time for me. I felt I needed to function well outwardly for so many people while inwardly I felt that God seemed to be completely silent to my needs. I continued to seek Him and yet I felt He could not be found. The intimacy I had once enjoyed with my God now seemed to escape me. This seemed contrary to what I believed the Bible said about Him. I suppose it was during this time that I began to question if in the silence, He was absent. Everything I had come to believe about Him was being challenged.

In His silence I felt desperate for Him. Contrary to my emotions or my reasoning, I came to realize later what a wonderful thing this silence was, and how it was as though He became an unseen magnet, drawing me to Him through my suffering. No words were spoken from Him, not even a *feeling* of hearing from Him, and yet I continued to be drawn by Him. No matter the degree of my despair, I felt I wanted to keep going until I had a greater understanding of Him. It was at this point that I chose to fight for my faith. It is true, I am a stubborn woman. I dug my feet of faith deep into the soil of all the truth I had yet learned of Him. I held desperately to all I had embraced about Him in the journey that had led me to this time. Please understand that I didn't do this bravely nor did I do it with spiritual boldness. Instead, I was a broken, depressed, and needy child of His. I cried out to Him because I was desperate for His touch.

There is a story documented in several of the gospels. It tells of a woman desperate for the same kind of touch I found that I was seeking from God. I discovered myself in her. I imagined that she too was at the end of seeking medical care, and had lost hope that there was anything that could be done for her. Here I had found a companion in the scriptures. I wanted to spend some time with her.

The biblical account tells us this woman had suffered from a bleeding disorder for twelve years and that she could not be healed by anyone. She had endured much at the hands of many physicians. She had spent all she had, and was not helped at all, but rather had grown worse.[31] Oh to have been able to sit at the local coffee shop and sip a latte' with this dear woman. At this point in my life I imagined that she and I could have really enjoyed one another's company, and would have no doubt spent hours together.

The scripture account of her story tells us that in addition to the financial loss from seeking treatment, she had also been excommunicated from any social circle. Because her disorder involved blood, she was considered to be unclean. In spite of this aloneness she exhibits faith. Oh my, how glorious for me to see this precious woman's story included in

---

31   "And a woman who had had a hemorrhage for twelve years, and had endured much at the hands of many physicians, and had spent all that she had and was not helped at all, but rather had grown worse." Mark 5:25-26 HCSB

the Bible! She is such an example of faith to me. I don't think this came easy for her, nor do I believe that it was an automatic response. I believe God was working in her life throughout the process of those many years and prepared her for her experience with Jesus. I also believe, like me, this lady had been on a long journey of faith that had brought her to the place where she now found herself standing.

She exhibited just the kind of faith I longed to exhibit. It was exactly the kind of "dig your heels in, and fight a battle to believe" kind of faith that I felt I was experiencing. For me it seems that this kind of faith is often manifested in one who by all outward appearances doesn't seem strong and exuberant. Often, great stories of those who show strong and even miraculous faith have been those much like this dear woman. Weary and desperate, she was quite an example for me.

I imagine in the long haul of twelve years of disability she had cried, felt alone, and experienced what seemed to be silence from God. I believe that when she arrived at the place where I found her in scripture, she had lost hope in any other source. I believe that she too had experienced some "broken-spirited days" just as I had. Yet, in the midst of her broken spirit she had continued on her journey and her pursuit of Jesus.

No matter what you may struggle with in your life, you can perhaps relate to this feeling. It may not even be a physical challenge that you yourself are confronting. Perhaps you have experienced isolation brought on you by other forces. Often those who experience divorce, financial failure, or loss of employment feel this type of isolation. Some of the life experiences that we face can cause us to feel that we no longer fit in with the norms of society. We struggle with attitudes and beliefs that we fear others will have about us.

This woman in scripture was considered unclean and unfit to be in the company of others. Oh how Satan uses this tactic within the thoughts we have about ourselves. There are times we may find that we are in a situation of our own making. At other times we are the victims of choices others have made. We may struggle as she did with a physical disorder that is beyond our control or we may struggle with something that has come about as the direct result of poor choices we have made. Whatever the reason, we may feel isolated, unworthy or simply unable to let others know the depth of what we are experiencing.

Satan just loves to work in our isolation. If he can convince us that we are unfit to be in the company of others, he has us in just the vulnerable place where he can attack us. In his hunt to destroy, he separates us from the pack. This is how he then devours our spirit. He seems to specialize in making us feel unfit. I encourage you dear one, do not fall prey to this tactic. See him for the liar that he is.[32] Regardless of the choices you have made, you need never to live in seclusion believing that you are too unfit for God's redemptive touch.

Our thoughts matter to God.

The encouragement to us all is the faith that this woman exhibits once she sees Jesus. Scripture tells us that she thought, "If I just touch His garments, I shall get well."[33] There is so much for us to consider in this small statement. Can you imagine? This woman's *thoughts* were so important they are actually noted in our God-breathed scriptures! Hear me when I say this. God cares about every thought that enters your mind. He is so opposed to Satan's view. God doesn't want you alone, isolated, and feeling unfit! For this account to give us such detail during a time in which women were considered to be no more than property, with little place of importance outside the home is simply astounding. If her thoughts mattered to the degree that they are told for all eternity in our scripture, hear me when I say to you, this is significant! Your thoughts matter to God.

This is a dear example to us of a woman who struggled, who lived in a circumstance not of her own choosing, and who desired to have a different life. She didn't want to live in isolation. She would not settle for a life of hopelessness. The challenge this woman faced is not what appears to have mattered most to God. Instead it was her thoughts and the faith she modeled. I believe that God had led her on a journey of faith for twelve long years to bring her to this day. Even if she had experienced times of questioning God or doubting that He was working on her behalf, her journey of faith had been refining her for this very moment. Her faith had grown through the years of emotional and physical pain. This faith now expresses itself with complete assurance that Jesus was the cure for her need.

---

32 "You are of your father the Devil, and you want to carry out your father's desires. He was a murderer from the beginning and has not stood in the truth, because there is no truth in him. When he tells a lie, he speaks from his own nature, because he is a liar and the father of lies." John 8:44 HCSB

33 For she said, "If I can just touch His robes, I'll be made well." Mark 5:28 HCSB

When she touched His garment expressing her confident faith and being fully assured that she would be healed, scripture tells us that "the flow of her blood was dried up." Jesus knew immediately that "power proceeding from Him had gone forth". What does Jesus say when He approaches her? "Daughter, your faith has made you well; go in peace, and be healed of your affliction". Had the kind of faith she exhibited been an automatic response? I don't think so. I believe this expression of faith was fruit born out of many years of tilling the soil of her heart and her beliefs about who she knew her God to be. In scripture she became a dear friend of mine. When I get to heaven I am anxious to meet her and tell her how her example of faith spurred me on at a time I could have felt defeat. If heaven does have latte's, prepare now to pull up a chair and share with this dear daughter of Christ who teaches us what real faith looks like.. I invite you dear one: come along with me in your journey. Don't remain in despair or trapped in Satan's lies. Fight for your faith! Your God is near and is tilling the soil of your spirit through whatever it is you may be facing. The cares of your heart are of great importance to Him.

Chapter Seven

☙

Healed For His Purposes

The Seeming Silence of God

Real faith is not expressed on the basis of what
we see. It expresses itself based upon what we
hope for. It believes in what it cannot see.

God had been tilling the soil of my heart and my own beliefs about Him
throughout my journey with disability. I, just like the woman who reached
for Jesus in the crowd, had been on a faith journey during my nearly
five years of infirmity. God seemed to be silent at a time I found myself
encountering thoughts of aloneness. The loss of hope that my situation
could change was now mixed with increased physical pain, and this pain
was almost more than I could bear. I clung to my Bible in such a way that
I thought surely my fingernail prints would become deeply ingrained as
handles in the leather cover. Even when I couldn't sense God's presence in
some of the ways I had earlier experienced, I continued to rest upon His
promise that He would never leave me or forsake me.[34] Often this was the
only truth I was able to call out to Him.

I knew that I must trust in all I had learned thus far. This is such an
important step, dear one. When you find that you are in the heat of the

---

34 "...for He Himself has said, I will never leave you or forsake you." Hebrews
13:5b HCSB

battle, and you feel the urge to retreat, you are closer to your victory than you realize. Though you may retreat from the people around you, know that God is there with you. Call out to Him all the truths you have come to know thus far about Him. Speak of them even if it seems that you are somewhat reminding God of who He is, as though He might not already know this. Take this time to offer an inventory of what you have learned thus far about who He is to you, and the power that He brings into your presence. This becomes your way of offering praise to Him in the midst of all you are facing. The Bible tells us that He inhabits the praise of His people.[35] You are letting Him know that you are trusting that He is there with you in spite of the aloneness you may feel. Assure Him that you are resting on every truth that He has given you. Speak your trust to Him in spite of what you might see with your eyes. The Bible teaches us that real faith is not expressed on the basis of what we see. It is instead faith that expresses itself based upon what we hope for. Faith believes in something it cannot see.[36]

> The one who confesses their sin is then
> able to receive from God.

If the circumstance or the feelings you are battling are the result of your own making rather than something beyond your control, then confess this to Him. Acknowledge before God the part you have played in the process that has brought you to where you are. The one who confesses their sin is able then to receive from God.[37] Once you have received His cleansing and forgiveness, recognize that you are just that. You have been washed clean of your sin, and God has both forgiven you and also forgotten your sin. He has moved on to redeeming you from the pit of despair and instead setting you firmly on a new path. Shift your focus to the great and awesome God who wants to act on your behalf.[38] In doing this, you will give Satan no room to work in your thoughts about yourself. As he seeks to assail you with disbelief or erode your confidence in who the scripture

---

35 "But You are holy, enthroned on the praises of Israel." Psalm 22:3 HCSB
36 "Now faith is the reality of what is hoped for, the proof of what is not seen." Hebrews 11:1 HCSB
37 "If we confess our sins, He is faithful and righteous to forgive us our sins and to cleanse us from all unrighteousness." I John 1:9 HCSB
38 "Blessed is the man who trusts in the LORD, whose confidence indeed is the LORD." Jeremiah 17:7 HCSB

says your God is, you are able to stand firm because you know His word is truth. His word says that if you confess, He forgives. As He forgives, He cleanses you. Counter any negative thoughts Satan will try to hurl at you with these truths. Satan will assail you with temptations to return to that pit of despair. When he does this, acknowledge that you are no longer on a journey with Satan and look for your way of escape.[39] This will give you peace.[40]

> Journaling your prayers can become a tool God will use to
> build your faith.
> The journal of prayers becomes a written testimony of
> God's activity.
> This will build your faith as you look
> back over your history with Him.

In my own journey of faith I began to journal my prayers. In the journaling of our prayers we can later see how God has been present and responding to our prayers. We may not fully see this on a day to day basis. The journal becomes a written testimony of His activity in our lives. It was in the journaling of my prayers that I could later see how God was in fact present, and responding to my prayers even though I felt alone.

I can't emphasize enough how much I encourage you to begin to journal your prayers. It need not be lengthy or worded in ways that may seem too difficult for you to do. It may only be a sentence or two. But if you will attempt this, it will become a wonderful tool that God can use to build your faith as you look back over your history with Him.

For me, journaling my prayers resulted in a very powerful testimony that God chose to later use. I had no way of knowing at the time I wrote those prayers that God would do an amazing thing in my life and use my feeble words to show Himself to be mighty. Although the pages in my journal were written without any thought at the time that they would ever be shared, I am compelled to share them as a testament to this truth. As

---

39 "No temptation has overtaken you except what is common to humanity. God is faithful and He will not allow you to be tempted beyond what you are able, but with the temptation He will also provide a way of escape, so that you are able to bear it." I Corinthians 10:13 HCSB

40 "Stand, therefore, with truth like a belt around your waist, righteousness like armor on your chest, and your feet sandaled with readiness for the gospel of peace." Ephesians 6:14-15 HCSB

you read my prayers you will see and hear my pain and aloneness as I cried out to God. I pray that as you hear my story you too will reach out for the hem of Jesus' garment in order to experience Him as you never have before. In doing so, you will grasp the greatness of God in the journey.

August, 2001...First Entry

"It is such a confusing time Lord. You move so powerfully in one way and so painfully in another. You lead me and open doors in my writing, and in my opportunities to minister to others. I sense you enlarging my territory of witness in so many ways, and yet, I am in the midst of such a painful time. The pain is physical (both in my shoulder and in my feet) and it is also emotional. It is so easy to praise you when doors are opening in ministry. At the same time I struggle to find your purpose in allowing my body to fail me. One thing I know. You are present in both!"

"I am unchanged in my love for you, unwavering in my trust in you, and undaunted in pursuing what is your vision of our future together. My struggle is not knowing how or where to seek relief for my pain, and direction for my disease. I don't even know how to word my prayer, and so I don't. I quietly lay before you. I hear only my sobs. Do you hear more? Does the spirit intercede in such a way that you hear the cry of my heart?"

"Thank you for brushing past me on Friday. When I did not have words for you, you had words for me. Thank you for speaking them out of the mouth of that tiny child of God. Only five or six years of age, she stood before me glowingly dressed in white with her beautiful white beaded braids. Her face gazed with the radiance of an angel. Her dark ebony skin contrasted the shining white of her beautiful smile. With her head held high she gazed into my eyes with angelic precision. When I complimented her beauty she proudly arched her back, stood tall, and exclaimed emphatically with the broadest of smiles, "I love God, and He loves me!"

"In the midst of all my pain, and despair, her words penetrated my sorrow bringing words to my prayers. If this tiny babe knew the only real truth that matters, I too knew that her sweet childlike faith had uttered words that would restore me."

"I love you Lord and I know you love me. No matter the circumstances or the pain, that truth alone will see me through it all."

August, 2001...Second Entry

"It is a good day, less pain. Lord, give me the faith to believe it is possible for me to be without pain. I have walked in and out of so many days with it that each one takes more and more of my hope. Yet, I know you are my hope. My hope is certainly not found in the medical community."

"Lord, so many are praying. Please don't let my lack of faith prevent answered prayer in their lives. I continue to increase the new medicine. Give me the wisdom to know and sense its effectiveness. Beyond all this, my dear Lord, let me see you. Show me how it all works together for your glory."

August, 2001...Third Entry

"More and more I am able to function with less pain. Thank you Lord. Please teach me all that you want me to know of you as Jehovah Rapha, my healer."

Three days following this last entry I went to work as I had on any other normal day. At the close of my day my husband arrived and we headed for home. As we entered the highway we were chatting with each other about our day. Up until that moment it had been a good day however I suddenly began to feel nauseated. We were in a van at the time and I told him to continue telling me about his day but I needed to recline the seat due to my nausea. The reclined seat only compounded what my stomach was already feeling, so I returned to an upright position. That thought is the last thing I remember about the ride home. Ray tells me that as I brought the seat up I fell over unconscious. We of course returned to the hospital where I worked.

I remember feeling a vague awareness of consciousness as hospital personnel took me from the van onto a stretcher. When I entered the emergency room I was awake but very tired. I remember hearing and feeling my husband and my friend Butch, remove my leg braces. After a series of tests it was determined that I needed to be admitted for further testing. I now jokingly say that this is how hospitals pay for all their equipment. In a short while, I was very glad that the equipment was available.

I felt very tired from the incident and just wanted to sleep. The next day I was frustrated to now be hospitalized for yet something else. A tilt table test was ordered. This is a test during which they would determine if my blood pressure remained stable during episodes of changed positions. It would also monitor how my heart responded. I failed the test miserably.

Neither my blood pressure nor my heart remained stable, and the technicians were forced to intervene with the drug, Atropine. This drug is administered in an emergency and increases the blood pressure while restoring the heart rate. I again was exhausted and wanted to sleep. I was told they would bring in a cardiologist to consult with me. In addition to my family practice doctor, I already had a neurologist, and certainly didn't want to add another specialist to my medical repertoire. The feeling that God had taken a day off seemed to engulf me.

On the second morning of my hospital stay, more than anything else, I wanted a bath! I was someone who always joked that a bath was like a religious experience. I enjoyed soaking in bubble-scented suds. I would often spend time with God alone in this solitude. He sees and knows all and I feel there is no need for apology to Him for how my body looks. After all, He is the one who created it! Well glory to God, there in the bathroom of my hospital room was a bathtub. It was not a shower but an actual tub. I decided I would take a bath. I reasoned that they wouldn't have that tub there if they didn't intend for me to use it. So I went into the bathroom, drew me a bath, and unsnapped my heart monitor buttons, as I prepared to get in. Well as you can imagine, I instantly had an audience! They explained how I couldn't unsnap my monitor buttons and I certainly couldn't have a bath. In the hospital a bath was defined as a plastic pan, a washcloth and a very generic bar of soap.

Two days after entering the hospital I received a card from the prayer ministry of my church. Someone had written to me in response to my earlier feelings and desperation for prayer. I want to share with you what this card said to me.

"Dear Pat, as I lift you up in prayer to our Lord, I know that He is the God of the impossible and that His power is above <u>all</u> we might know or understand. I pray that our Lord would not only return wholeness to your shoulder but I step beyond that and in His loving power I seek complete healing for you. To God be the Glory!" These prayer cards remain anonymous so I may never know until I reach heaven exactly who it was that encouraged me so deeply with these words. What great faith this person extended on my behalf and I am forever grateful that someone was willing to take time out from the hectic pace of their life, and go to the prayer room for one such as me.

Throughout the week various test were completed and the cardiologist said that he wouldn't be surprised if I purchased a pacemaker before going home. There were many things I wanted to purchase but a pacemaker wasn't on my list. Throughout the week I had a couple more incidents that all required Atropine. When the final diagnosis was made, I had a serious case of something called Neuro-Cardiogenic Syncope. People who have this may typically feel faint for no apparent reason. In my case, once the vagus nerve reflex was triggered within my body, then my blood pressure would drop to dangerously low levels. I was put on medication and told if I could go two days without an incident I could go home. I called upon everyone to pray so that I could return to home, normal activities, and of course, a long and sudsy bath.

I did in fact make it through the next two days without incident and without the need for further Atropine intervention. On that Monday morning, one week after entering the hospital, I was preparing to go home. A nurse entered my room and we began a conversation about my care. Suddenly, I felt faint and I quickly lost consciousness. Little did I realize then how God was in my room and was about to make Himself known in a very powerful way.

When sharing my story I always stop here to tell listeners I realize that what I am about to share with you may seem unusual. You would be correct to see it that way. It was anything but usual. For some reason God allowed me in my unconsciousness to be aware of my surroundings and what was going on in my room. I was not floating over the bed and there was no light at the end of the tunnel. I do not dismiss others stories of such accounts. Those just were not mine. Although my eyes were closed, I could see.

I saw that the furniture had been pushed back, and my bed was angled with the head of my bed to the floor, and the foot of the bed in the air. It was later explained to me that this position allowed for the blood to flow to my heart. What is known as the "crash cart", the mobile unit brought to a bedside to revive one's heart, was now positioned to my left. I knew then that my condition was serious. I was surrounded by a team of nurses, technicians, and a doctor. Because I worked at the hospital I recognized them to be the code blue team. This code is called when no pulse is evident.

I always tell people that they really should train doctors to have a more hopeful face during a code blue. When you are surrounding a critically ill patient you really never can be certain of what they are seeing and hearing. My doctor was leaning with one arm against the wall and the other arm was extended, running his hand through his hair as he directed orders for medications. He had a very worried look on his face. There were various lines of equipment extending from me and certainly, my body gave reason for concern.

The nurse whom I had been having conversation with was now kneeling beside my bed. The bedrails were down and she was attempting to administer medication into my IV line. With the bed rail down and my arms extended off to the sides, my face was ashen and my lips were blue. I heard her call out, "I have no line…I have no line!" I had slept during the night in my usual position with my hands under my pillow. Apparently I had dislodged my IV line during the night. I was well aware of the struggle nurses routinely encountered with my veins and so as they gave needles to her, I knew my time was limited. The reality of my situation was clear to me. At that moment I prepared to meet Jesus. I believed that within seconds the One whom I had sought so desperately to intimately know and understand would reach for me and we would gaze upon each other face to face.

When one encounters this type of experience they fleetingly feel a host of emotions. I can tell you that while all of this was happening very fast it seemed to be almost in slow motion to me. I had never before faced the imminent reality of meeting my Jesus. There has only been one perfect person who lived a life without sin and He is Jesus. It matters not who we are; all of us when faced with imminent death may feel that we have some house cleaning to do, and certainly I was no exception.

I also remember feeling sad that I was going to leave my husband and my children. As a mother I didn't feel the job was completed in raising my daughter and two sons. There was so much more for Ray and I to enjoy together and the thought of him being alone in it was sad for me. Then as if in the spirit, I relaxed with a peace that can only come from God. I realized then that this is truly the moment we live our life for. I rested deeply waiting to see Him.

Suddenly I heard the nurse say, "I have a line; a blind stick, I'm in." Then with no visual awareness but with a deep spiritual consciousness, God powerfully made His presence known to me in the room. My feet which were extended upward to Him became as fire. This was not just a stinging sensation but truly they felt as though they were on fire. I became conscious though very sedated. They were saying, "we have to get her to intensive care…we cannot monitor her here." The next awareness I had was of Ray and my best friend standing there with me. I reached for my friend trying desperately to express to her what she meant to me and wanting assurance that she would care for my children. I felt the cool air brushing

74

over me as I was speedily rolled into the intensive care unit. Clearly, neither home nor a sudsy bath would come that day.

I was immediately being hooked to a host of machines while shiny foil-like pads were placed strategically upon my chest in the event that I should code. My mouth was so dry due to the high doses of medication that had been given to me and I wanted desperately to talk. Ray stood beside me looking so frightened. He stroked my arm as I desperately tried to relay to him how much I loved him. I wanted him to know what a gift it was to me that at that time in our marriage there was nothing I felt I needed to make right with him. Friends, I know you know that this is not always true for us. We live each day with little thought that it could be our last. Consider this today. Love those around you as though it were your last chance to make them see, hear, and be embraced in your love.

Both the cardiologist and the neurologist came in. I was told that my condition would not cause my death but that I was there for monitoring. I was able to ask that they put the pacemaker in and was told they could not do that. The insurance company would not allow it! The cardiologist explained that due to the cost of a pace-maker they had to prove that medication had failed. At that moment I certainly felt I had proven this but they did not. My medications were doubled and I remained in intensive care for three days.

On the second day Butch was sitting with me while my family went to eat dinner. In intensive care you don't do many things for yourself. Because of being hooked to so many lines of medical technology I was unable to move easily in the bed. I asked my friend to take the covers off my feet because my feet were hot. This was quite unusual due to my disease. My feet had always been cold and without any color. When she pulled the covers back they were pink and warm to touch. I began to move my toes; something I had not done for nearly four years. We both instantly looked at one another and began praising God. She even went out and bought nail polish to paint my toenails making them pretty as people would now see them move in ways they had not moved. Neither she nor I realized then the scope of what God had done for me.

I suffered no more incidents and was returned to the telemetry unit where I had previously been. I was told that if I went twenty-four hours without an incident I would be able to go home. The nurse came in to take me for a walk down the hall. She explained how getting up and walking was a requirement before going home. She stated that if I was to have an incident, it would probably be when I got up and moved about. You can imagine her excitement at being the nurse assigned to this task.

I did not have my braces at the hospital. It had been ten days since I had been brought in through the emergency room. I jokingly tell how I put on the little $750.00 sock-like slippers they "give" you at the hospital. The nurse stood beside me, and as I stood to walk, I knew without any doubt that God had healed me. I had complete control and support in my feet. The ways that my brain had become somewhat disconnected to my feet had now changed. I had a complete sense of where my feet were. I looked at the nurse and glowingly said, "I've been healed!" She confusingly looked back and said, "You've been what?" Now you really would think a nurse would be familiar with the term *healed*, wouldn't you? As I explained, she of course realized what I was saying had happened. She seemed to accept my words albeit with a limited belief as she urged me on out the room. I gleefully walked the entire length of the hospital hallway without incident. The excitement was overwhelming for me.

Suddenly I realized where our walk had taken us in the hallway. When we walked past the room where I had previously experienced the code blue incident, I truly felt I was standing at a holy place. I turned and quietly said to the nurse, "I must pause here." She had no knowledge that this had been my previous room and certainly didn't realize the magnitude of emotion I felt. I knew that God had entered that room blazing a trail of His glory. The fact that my body had been a venue of His incredible and glorious power both humbled and astounded me. I felt like I wanted to dance. She calmed me and led me back to my bed. She exited my room and I lay silently weeping before Him. The contrast of what I had once felt, weeping during the times of His silence and now tears of joy that I shed, brought me to such a place of humility before my God. It was for me, the sweetest time of worship I have ever had with Him.

Later that afternoon I called friends who had been such vital prayer partners with me over the years. I also called my husband and children telling them all to come to the hospital at 4:30 p.m. because I had something special to show them. They all came having no idea of the glorious news I was about to share. When they arrived, I waltzed into the hallway walking with no braces. I stopped short and spinning around I said to them, "are you going to follow me?"

I truly felt that my body was a display of the power of our God! What was before us was Jesus incarnate, in my flesh; the revealed glory of Him! Everyone stood motionlessly lined across the hallway; each of them stunned, and in tears. Just days before, I had been surrounded by each of them as they hovered over my intensive care bed. All of us were uncertain as to how God could be working in this. Now we returned to my room and oh what a praise service we held for our God! He had seemed silent or even absent to me during that long first night all alone in intensive care. When I had been rolled into the intensive care unit, the bed had been latched and locked into position. Satan had hurled assailing darts into my thoughts as I lay alone listening to the beeping of the monitors. Over and over again the liar whispered, "You will never leave here alive." Over and over again I whispered to God, "You are here, you will not leave me alone." I sensed no response from God. He seemed silent. Oh, but dear one, He was anything but absent.

> The seeming silence of God should
> never be mistaken as absence.

There are times we experience what seems to us as complete silence from God. Let me say to you dear one, never mistake this for absence. Worship Him in the silence as though you are staring at Him face to face, for truly you are. My healing was never expected and I now live every moment of my life to fulfill the purpose for which He chose to give it. Whether I am crippled or whether I am not, I glory in the great God who loves, never abandons, and who is always working for my good. Glory to His name!

Chapter Eight

He Heals Me, He Heals Me Not

*Holding to Your Faith When It Seems That God
Choices to Heal Some, While Others He Does Not.*

As God responds to our prayers, fulfilling His purpose,
His intent is not to always give us what we want.

Why is not everyone for whom we pray, healed? Wouldn't it seem logical that if God is known as the "Great Physician", then all could be healed? Because not everyone who seeks healing receives it, and some with the need for healing have prayed fervently to God asking for that, it's a fair question to ask. There have probably been those who have even lost faith in the power of God through an experience of seeking Him for healing and not receiving it. Others may have held to their faith but continued on with a somewhat confused understanding of this aspect of God's character and identity.

The process of confronting any health dilemma evokes a host of emotions. It also involves medical opinions, technology, and exposure to educational resources. It can all be overwhelming. It certainly was for me! The host of emotions I confronted seemed to collide with the realities of my physical condition. At that intersection of emotions there was also all the information and treatments coming at me. I think the person who confronts a physical or mental malady naturally desires the return of good health.

The process of seeking healing is complex. The many complicated issues that arise throughout a diagnosis and treatment also presents such considerations as age and severity of illness. Physicians often use the phrase: "Risk v's Advantage." Sometimes the risk of treatment is greater than the advantages that treatment might offer. There is also an arena of public opinion regarding the importance placed upon physical healing in light of a given situation. For example, the need for physical healing might be weighted more heavily when a young parent or a child is stricken with a terminal disease. But in the case of one who has lived long years, and experienced life abundantly, we may still feel a host of emotions, yet be better able to accept a diagnosis that seemingly will end their life. This circumstance becomes one in which we gather around the individual in love, care, and support. Our pursuit becomes one of easing pain, and offering comfort as we find peace in knowing they are ending well in their journey of life.

When I was younger I was employed at an area nursing home. Needless to say, most of the residents that came to live with us had moved there as the final residence along their journey of life. I was afforded the opportunity to be a part of the experiences of many families as they found themselves at the close of one's life here on earth. When death seemed imminent, families would often center their grief in those final hours around the loss of future experiences with their family member. No matter the age and how great the life their loved one had lived, they grieved the passing not only of the individual, but also the passing of the relationship their life had represented.

It is this harsh reality of death that forces us to realize that no matter how wonderful time spent with someone has been, it cannot last endlessly here on earth. While families I encountered faced sadness, I rarely saw them seek physical healing from God for an elderly person whose health had failed. Often they had already witnessed a gradual loss of all the things their loved one had once enjoyed. Certainly this absence of prayer for healing was no indicator of their love and devotion. It was simply a resignation to the truth that we are not made to endure eternally here on earth. This truth seemed to be easier to accept when one had grown old, and their body systems had deteriorated.

On the contrary, we also had residents who came to live with us during the final stages of a terminal disease. There were those who suffered cancer that had metastasized to vital organs. Some had brain tumors that were inoperable and would take their life after destroying their abilities to speak, or care for themselves in normal ways. Some had inherited diseases that had invaded their bodies and gradually robbed them of the ability to function as a part of their families at home. Still others were people who had lived high-risk lifestyles that had ensnared them and brought about their demise.

Many of these had just begun to live life to the fullest. Some were married with young children whom they no longer had the ability to recognize when they would come to visit. Others were highly successful business people who had left behind great careers and the promise of a bright future. In nearly every case there were family members who loved them, and could not abandon their pursuit of praying to God, asking Him to intervene in their circumstance, and give to them a miracle of healing.

In such cases of young, vibrant lives being struck down, it would seem natural for one to assume that a God of love would certainly want to answer their prayers, bring healing, and restore their families. In none of these particular cases did this occur. There were no earthly healings and no physical restorations. After great suffering each of them died.

So how then does the person who has put their faith in God come to a place of understanding why it is that He doesn't always give the type of healing we are seeking from Him? It becomes for them a choice of either abandoning faith in their God, or seeking to know His ways on a level that is far deeper than their typical way of thinking.

Many of us learned at an early age to bow our heads, and begin our prayer at mealtime with these words, "God is good, God is great." Most people in society seem to grow up to be orderly, logical thinkers. We grow to assume that if something seems unfair to us - such as a young mother or father being struck down by tragedy or disease, then this God, who is both good and great, will naturally want to stop the seeming unfairness of it. A good and great God would never want to stand idly by and not intervene. After all, He is God! Jesus Himself, states in the Bible that everything is possible with God.[41] And so we often believe when we pray, God not only can heal but that He will. Then when He does not, we are shaken in the faith we have placed in One who by all appearances to us, has not lived up to His name. How can we believe that God is good while we cling desperately to the one we love and do not want to live without?

---

41 He replied, "What is impossible with men is possible with God." Luke 18:27 HCSB

How can we believe He is great as we hold the one we love and feel life slipping from their body?

> In any given circumstance of our life God is working for our good; even when we cannot see and understand this.

I had experienced times in my own life in which I had sought God in prayer, asking Him to give healing, and restore health in the life of one whom I loved. My father had faced a terminal cancer diagnosis at fifty-nine years of age. I wanted very much to continue to have him as a part of my life. As a young mother I knew that if he died, my preschool children would have no memory of him. His battle with cancer lasted less than two years and he ultimately succumbed to the disease in spite of treatment and a host of prayers. The journey through that time was for me a great journey of faith.

As I had prayed for the healing of my dad, I found it difficult to understand the truth that God was working for our good. When you see the health of one you love fading away, taking with it piece by piece all their abilities, and you watch the personality of the one you love fade into silence, it can be a challenge of faith to believe that God is working. I didn't feel that what I was witnessing could be defined as His good work. Certainly I didn't see it as an answer to my prayers for his healing. Those prayers were the strongest weapon I had against this ravaging cancer, and that didn't seem to be working, I felt hopeless.

This is a place that many people of faith may find they are in. Perhaps you feel you are in this place even as you read these words. Let me say to you dear one, just as God is not absent in times that seem like silence to us, He also is never off the job. Even at times that seem like He isn't responding as we desire, God is always working in our midst. His work is always for a good outcome. He is always about the business of bringing good out of all that concerns us.[42]

How can this be so? God did not allow the health of my dad to be restored. He didn't give healing in the way I had expected Him to give. All of my children have grown into adulthood and have none of the wonderful memories their grandfather would have made with them. Their knowledge of him is solely based on pictures and stories they have heard. My mother was left as a widow at forty-nine years of age. She felt so alone

---

42 "We know that all things work together for the good of those who love God; those who are called according to His purpose." Romans 8:28 HCSB

and frightened about her future. How could these things be seen as the goodness of God working in our lives?

My prayers for my father's healing were a great part of the faith journey God has allowed me to travel with Him. It was long before my own personal healing, and certainly long before I had learned to put my complete trust in God's sovereign control. To say that God is sovereign means that He has supreme authority. For me to surrender this place of control and give God this supreme authority over my life first meant that I had to recognize that He was deserving of this place. Jesus, when speaking to His disciples, for the final time before His ascension into heaven, said to them, "All authority has been given to me in heaven and on earth." Matthew 28:18a HCSB. He was the creator of the universe and all that it contained.[43]

Second, it meant that because He was the creator and I was His creation, it was He who had the knowledge, and skill to oversee that which He had made. This knowledge and skill was deserving of my respect and honor. He had the power to act on my behalf and to do so in a just and trustworthy manner.[44] I had to put my trust in His knowledge and honor Him with my respect.

I needed to truly surrender to His authority and control. For me it was surrendering a critical spirit towards God for the outcome of circumstances, and instead, seeking wisdom and understanding about His ways. There is a vast difference between criticism and the pursuit of understanding. God loves for his children to seek Him and desire to understand Him in a greater way. It is our approach that matters to Him.

We must come to Him with a trust and confidence in His sovereignty, never forgetting that He is a Holy God. We must surrender the need to know why He allows some things to occur in our life. In this surrender we acknowledge before Him all we know, and have learned of His character, prior to that time in our journey. In acknowledging who we know God to be, He meets us at that place and continues to build on our knowledge of Him. As He does this we will recognize that though we do not understand, He is still traveling the journey with us. In this journey it is He who is the tour guide. We can have no better guide, my friend. After all, He created everything in our world and continues to sustain it all. It is a journey I will

---

43 "In the beginning, God created the heavens and the earth." Genesis 1:1 HCSB

44 "For I will proclaim the LORD'S name. Declare the greatness of our God! The Rock – His work is perfect; all His ways are entirely just. A faithful God, without prejudice, He is righteous and true." The Song of Moses - Deuteronomy 32:3-4 HCSB

continue to travel with my Lord until that day when I meet Him face to face. There are times I am elated with His presence and the beauty of all He brings into my life. There are other times however when that elation is not there. The scenery is not always pretty. Let me share with you one turn in the road that remains for me a place that God and I spent a lot of time together. During this time I was seeking to understand the Lord's thoughts about healing and He no doubt wanted to share them with me.

You can imagine that for me it had been a great time of elation during the weeks following my own personal healing and the removal of any need to ever again wear my braces. When Ray brought me home from the hospital, I sat on the side of my bed, all alone in our bedroom. It was so wonderful to finally be home after a two-week hospital stay that had turned my life into anything but normal.

Sitting there savoring the smell of home, and the hum of life about me, brought such a feeling of contentment. As I glanced about the bedroom my eyes took in everything that made up the personal relationship Ray and I had enjoyed. Slowly as my eyes scanned the room I glanced at our shared closet, the photos of our life together, and the spot where he always left his clothes. Each place became for me a silent testimonial of what would have been left behind had things turned out differently.

Then my eyes locked onto the most riveting testimonial of all. There in their usual resting place lay the cumbersome braces that had once weighted not only my legs, but my heart, and my spirit. I began to weep at their presence. I knew they would no longer need their resting place. Their burdensome hold upon my body had been loosed and I had been set free from the weighty emotions that had surrounded me whenever I wore them. All pain was gone! It was almost too much for me to take in.

The weeks following my hospital stay were spent building my strength and re-entering normal life. I needed a lot of solitude during the first days of this time period. I felt so humbled before God; so undeserving of such a touch from Him. I wasn't able to put a great number of words to my prayers as I tried to express to Him my gratitude. As I would begin to pray, I would simply weep and utter, "Precious...precious...Savior."

After growing stronger both in body and in spirit, I decided that I was ready to be in a crowd and embrace my church friends. A church banquet was being held and I decided the evening would be a good opportunity for me to be with so many of the people who had prayed for me. They had heard of my healing but had not seen me. I decided of course, like any self-respecting woman, to go shopping for a new outfit. I had no shoes other than the lace-up gym shoes that I had worn over the years. Ray wanted to go with me to select dress shoes. This was something I had not worn for nearly five years. It was quite an emotional shopping trip. Honestly, we cradled those shoes as if we had adopted twins.

That evening we were surrounded by such jubilant, celebratory friends, and as I turned at one point to sit down, my eyes glanced up and there he was. Mike came bounding across the room with his usual swaying walk. He threw his arms around me and as he hugged me, he kept saying, "I can't believe it, I just can't believe it." Here was the friend God had placed beside me that first evening, sitting on the patio, brokenhearted at the prospect of wearing braces. That strong, confident man, who sipped tea with me totally unashamed at the presence of his amputated leg and the steel-like post that now served as his leg. The contrast of these two evenings seemed overwhelming. We celebrated a great banquet at church together as all of us gathered around the table rejoicing, laughing, and living life to the fullest. None of us could have been prepared for what lay ahead.

Three weeks after that evening Mike entered the hospital for what was to be a routine operation for the removal of his spleen. He had not felt well for some time and had begun a host of testing procedures. When the surgeons opened his abdomen his body was full of a cloudy fluid. It was believed that Mike had Mesothelioma a cancer caused by exposure to asbestos. A host of test would prove this to be true.

I could hardly believe we were standing at his bedside. He had bound into my jubilant celebration just weeks before, celebrating my healing with his big hug and his loud words exclaiming, "I just can't believe it!" Now, I had those same words pouring out of me as I watched this horror unfold. I could not believe where we were. My body felt numb inside as I sought to be a friend to my dear sister in Christ, who had stood so faithfully with me just weeks earlier. Reflecting back on that time, I thought back to my own hospital stay and could not put out of my mind the memory of my experience in intensive care. Three chairs sat at the end of my bed. Ray, Butch, and Mike occupied those chairs. Mike had left his job and had come immediately when he heard of my condition. I lay groggily realizing all the more how dear he and she were to Ray and me. None of us at that time knew what God had done in my body. It was Mike who had sat silently with me on that patio years before as I reeled from the reality of bulky braces intruding into my life, and it was he who sat quietly encouraging Ray in that intensive care unit. When the time came for them to leave, he came to my side and with hands coarsely engrained from work, he touched my cheek, giving me what was the only kiss I would ever receive from him. He whispered, "You'll be alright." Without asking me, he had known the fear I was feeling. Several days later when I discovered my healing as I walked, I could hardly wait to share it with him. I believe to this day that he had been as awestruck as I was. The contrast now felt between the joy of my news and the crushing sorrow of his seemed inexplicably unfair.

Now the roles were reversed as Mike lay in the same intensive care unit I had been in. His bed was only two cubicles away from the place where he had sat at the foot of my bed. I could hardly take in what was happening. His health deteriorated rapidly and at every turn I felt hope slipping away. My dear friend, Butch who had stood beside me in that same intensive care unit, and painted my toenails so my healing would look pretty, now stood brokenhearted at her husband's bedside. We each numbly glared at the other and I sought desperately to sustain hope in the midst of every doctor's despairing words. The pumping sound of the ventilator keeping time with the beeping of monitors left us speechless.

During this time I desperately went to God. I pleaded for understanding and for purpose. I couldn't fathom why He would choose this path in the journey. To plummet from extreme joy into a pit of agony caused me to cling to my God. He was the rock in the midst of a storm I couldn't even begin to categorize. I prayed as never before. All the while Mike's health deteriorated. His skin color grew ashen and all attempts to wean him from the ventilator were met with failure. Sounds of those machines still cause me to cringe.

Slipping alone into the room late one night, I stood alone with him, at the worst of times, and held his hand. Knowing that the drugs were so intense that he probably could not hear my words, I sobbed before God. I begged Him to do for Mike what He had done for me. He was the same unchanging God that He had always been. He had made Himself known to me in such dramatic ways and I had placed my confidence and trust in His sovereignty through so many different challenges. I knew that He was able to heal Mike, and I pleaded that He would do so. I even bargained with Him, telling Him that He could take back my healing and give it to Mike. I felt desperate and reached out to God as if there were some sort of heavenly bartering system I could engage in with Him. There was not, and only weeks after entering the hospital, Mike met Jesus face to face at just fifty-three years of age.

The scenery on this part of the faith journey was not pretty. I had no understanding of why God would choose to allow me to share jubilantly a dramatic healing yet He seemed to be unwilling to do so for Mike. I felt guilty that my life would go on in such a positive way and now my dear friend's life would be entrenched in the heartache that surrounds the loss of a spouse. How possibly could God be working for good in both of our lives?

> God does not always bring us to a place of understanding
> the good in our circumstance according to our timetable.

How does the one who faces the seemingly unjust scenario like I have described grow in their faith and become able to trust that God is working on their behalf? How can they trust even when the events of life seem unjust? I can speak to you only out of my own experience of walking with God on my personal faith journey. I can tell you that one cannot come to this kind of trust in God without pouring themselves into His word and continuing to build upon all they have learned of Him thus far. This is what our faith journey is for us.

In all of life we will come to see that our experiences are stepping stones in the journey with our God. Please understand that I do not mean to trivialize your pain by referring to it as a stepping stone. I realize that there are horrific tales of violence, disease, and life-altering events that can hardly be equated with something as small as a stepping stone. I have personally supported and prayed with many who have walked a journey of faith through things I could never imagine enduring. I want you to see that, for me personally, it was a part of my journey to either abandon the God who I could have decided wasn't trustworthy or push with faith, through the horror of these events, in order to continue to pursue a deeper relationship.

We come to that deeper relationship only if we allow Him to enter into our suffering. Although it is true that we may turn our backs, and abandon Him, He never abandons us.[45] He makes Himself known to us in the quiet moments spent with Him as we talk it out or cry with him through prayer, and as we read his word. I believe that the reason so many of us spend great amounts of time never moving further in our understanding of His ways is that the cost of such a relationship is just too great. We want a deep and intimate relationship with God but we want it to come rapidly, and without searching. The pursuit to know Him intimately takes both time

---

45 "...He Himself has said, I will never leave you or forsake you." Hebrews 13:5b HCSB

and commitment. We want the pleasure of His company without sacrifice. It requires the turning away from other things we seek to bring us comfort. It requires facing the pain and talking it out with God.

I pray as I write these words, that no matter where you may find yourself in your journey, you will take the time to honestly evaluate where you feel you are in your present pain. Perhaps you are as one of these family members I have mentioned. Perhaps the circumstance in your life seems overwhelmingly unfair and you feel deeply angry that a loving God would have chosen to allow such a thing to occur. You may feel you are unable to even consider talking with Him. I pray that you will allow me the undeserved privilege of coming to your side through my words right now.

Dear one, I want to say to you first that I understand where you are, because I too have felt some of the emotions you may be feeling. I want to say to you that I care deeply if you have tearfully surrendered to the emotions of anger and loss. My heart is compassionate towards those who have lost hope that they will ever feel joy again.

You may be stiffly keeping your chin up and functioning in ways that you must, all the while knowing that your pain is so deep, and so raw, that you could never let one such as me into your hurting soul. I am here to tell you that I know that pain. I understand the emotions that seem to snatch away any hope that you will ever feel differently than you do now. I know the desire to close the blinds and pull the covers of life over your head, and not let anyone know of your true aching heart.

Your story, just as many I have heard, may be so horrifically worse than mine, but I come alongside you to tell you the good news that we are not alone. Hear me my friend; we are not alone! God Himself is sitting here with us. Nothing can separate us from Him.[46] He knows the great hurt you are feeling. He is fully aware of any blame you may want to place upon Him for it. He is aware when your soul cries out, "Lord, you could have.... Father, if only you would have…Oh God, what I am bearing is so unfair!" He sees your heart completely and knows the weight of every emotion you are feeling. He is able to bear it, dear one. He is the only One who knows what it is like to bear the weight of the world.

---

46 "For I am persuaded that neither death nor life, nor angels nor rulers, nor things present, nor things to come, nor powers, nor height, nor depth, nor any other created thing will have the power to separate us from the love of God that is in Christ Jesus our Lord!" Romans 8:38-39 HCSB

He bore a great weight for both you and me upon a cross on a hill called Calvary. It was love that caused Him to be willing to receive those nails upon that cross. Was it fair? Did it seem to be a just act that the one who had never sinned would step forward, be willing to bear both the pain of a violent death, and the horror of hell, so that I would not have to experience what I deserved? Certainly it wasn't a fair or a just act, but it was done because He sees now what He can accomplish in your life if you will but allow Him to do it. He also sees the victory we will one day embrace and fully understand. He is so patient with us. Regardless of our emotions, He lovingly sits with us through it all. Often His presence is quiet and there in ways we don't even see or acknowledge. As we allow Him to enter into our pain, He continues to work for our good.

Please know dear one, God has an eternity time-table. His days are not as ours are.[47] He will wait patiently for you and never give up on the great plan He has for you. He took the first step when He left the glory of heaven and the splendor of His Father's presence and came to earth for you. He waits for you to take the next step to embrace Him in spite of your pain. It is true that there will be things which we will never understand completely until He brings us into His presence for all eternity with Him.

If we lose the day to day relationship with Him because we demand an understanding here on earth, we truly are the losers. I believe that the realization of eternity and the magnitude of its glory will have its effect on us in direct proportion to the trust we placed in Him during our days upon this earth.[48] Jesus is coming again, my friend, and He is bringing with Him His rewards.[49] I do not want to meet my Jesus in heaven, and only know Him as an acquaintance. I want to know Him intimately. Truly, I want to know Him as my very best friend and I have placed my faith in the promise that this is possible.[50] This truth has enabled me to come to

---

47 "Dear Ones, don't let this one thing escape you: with the Lord one day is like 1,000 years, and 1,000 years like one day." 2 Peter 3:8 HCSB

48 "Now without faith it is impossible to please God, for the one who draws near to Him must believe that He exists and rewards those who seek Him." Hebrews 11:6 HCSB

49 "See, the Lord GOD comes with strength, and His power establishes His rule. His reward is with Him, and His gifts accompany Him." Isaiah 40:10 HCSB

50 "No one has greater love than this, that someone would lay down his life for his friends. You are My friends if you do what I command you. I do not call you slaves anymore, because a slave doesn't know what his master is doing. I have called you friends, because I have made known to you everything I have heard from My Father." John 15:13 HCSB

a place of personally trading my pain and sorrow for His promises. Did I get full understanding? Certainly, I did not. But oh did I get a best friend in Jesus throughout the process! Someday I too will leave this earthly dwelling on a day of God's choosing. Surely, I look forward to meeting many of my family and friends there but the greatest of all will be when I meet my best friend; my Jesus. I know that I will see and understand then what I cannot now embrace. And so, I continue on the journey, holding fast to the One who says, He will never let me go.

Chapter Nine

Faith Steps into the Unknown

Learning to Trust God Enough to Step Out in Faith

God never does or allows one thing in our lives
without it having a purpose for another thing.

Following the extreme height of joy in my healing, coupled with the depth of loss in Mike's death, I found myself at a juncture in my life. Returning to normal activities seemed anything but normal. My body wasn't the same and death had again altered my circle of friends. Still, with these monumental changes came an ever present awareness; God was doing a new thing. This awareness seemed to engulf my every thought. Because this new thing included both joy *and* sadness, it created within me a spirit of deep conflict. Throughout those long days absorbed in these thoughts, I became acutely aware that God was drawing me into times of personal reflection of who He had already revealed Himself to be. In some ways it seemed much like a spiritual inventory of sorts. While this reflection brought great joy in the realization of just how much God had brought me through, the joy was mingled with the sadness of losing Mike. Yet life continued on, still demanding my participation. I had full confidence God was leading me on in my faith journey and I was determined to place my trust in this fact.

Returning to my workplace without braces had brought such a visual change of appearance. Co-workers were taken aback by it. Countless conversations about what I had experienced offered numerous opportunities to speak to others about the God I knew. During my times of quiet meditation, all alone with God, it became very clear to me; He never does or allows one thing in a life without it having a purpose for another thing. I have found that both our suffering and our joys are often entwined in the lives of others. I think God has purpose in this. I believe that whatever He allows in our life, those events become a means of revealing more of Himself, not only to us but also to someone else. Our lives will often become living expressions of God's purposes and also His provisions.

Wrestling with conflicted emotions, these quiet times with God became my solace. It was evident that this walk of faith was now taking me into new territory. Consequently, I dug in deep with the God whom I had trusted. I began to reflect back over my life. Pondering all the things God had done, I came face to face once again with the truth that my sovereign God had a purpose for all that had happened. I found myself again at a place of surrender. Either I would embrace His sovereignty or choose to question my faith in Him.

In complete humility, I was deeply moved not only by God's work but also by the enjoyable relationship into which He had drawn me. Equally so, I felt unworthy of such a great healing. I wanted to trust His sovereignty, yet a torrent of guilt flooded from my soul. I had lived through my medical trial. Not only had I lived, but also had received God's healing. All of this goodness in my life was being celebrated in the face of my friend, Butch who now faltered alone and without her husband. Feeling an overwhelming guilt that my life had so much joy while hers was marked with such raw grief, I struggled. Although she tried in every way to release me from feeling this guilt, my heart ached both for the loss of Mike and the happiness that could not be felt.

To appear joyful in the face of her sorrow seemed callous. While she celebrated with me and encouraged me to do the same, I felt that my happiness would rip open the wound of her hurting heart. My life had been changed through a miraculous healing while hers was forever changed through an indescribable death. I had something great come into my life while hers appeared robbed. Was God in fact working in our lives through these completely opposite emotions? Certainly He wanted goodness for us both, and yet nothing about her life and the journey she now traveled modeled goodness. What purpose might God have in working simultaneously in our lives through both gladness and sorrow? If He was working and had purpose in that process, I needed to understand how.

My perception of God and His activity
around me is never accurate enough for me to
presume what God is capable of doing.

Earlier in my journey with God and especially during the difficult years of my handicap, I found my time with the Lord had been full of questioning. Unlike those earlier days, I now had few words. I sat quietly in meditation and simply let His spirit flood my thoughts, my memories, and the life journey He had walked with me. There had been times in which God seemingly carried me along when I just felt too weak to continue on with Him. My quiet times of reflection continued, as days became weeks and weeks became months. I realized more than ever that my perception of God and His activity around me is never accurate enough for me to presume what He is capable of doing. My observation of God's greatness and His ability to work miraculously had relegated God to a place where my scope of belief was limited. This began to change dramatically. At the forefront of my thoughts and prayers there remained a deep revelation of His greatness, His intense abiding love, and trustworthiness. While I certainly didn't understand fully the course or the direction God was leading, I most definitely found Him to faithfully speak to me through His Word. These were the times that kept me seeking to understand Him and not cease the pursuit of truly knowing Him. Nothing is more precious than to experience this intimacy with God.

The splendor of God is not only revealed in times of joy
and happiness.
His triumphant majesty is equally present
in times of loss and sadness.

Throughout that year of great transition for myself as well as my dear friend, I would often recall memories of being both in the pit of despair, and also at the mountaintop of rejoicing. Reflecting back on how God had worked in times past gave me the encouragement to continue on the incredible thing I call "my faith journey." How comforting it was to embrace the sovereignty of God all over again. He truly had been the same all-knowing and powerful God, regardless of changing circumstances. It was true that throughout earlier years, God had been at work in my life forming foundations along the way. He no doubt had allowed all that occurred during the preceding decade of my life to become opportunities for bringing Him the greatest glory. Those events had allowed me to see that the splendor and triumphant majesty of God are equally present in times of joy and happiness, as well as times of deep sorrow.

Yes, there were times in which I felt completely helpless and unable to respond to God. Even now, there are those times which make no sense to my finite mind. In those times, I am once again confronted with the sovereignty of a triumphant God. I do not always understand His ways, and certainly I will never be able to fully grasp His thoughts. Still, I am completely convinced that God loves. I am ever mindful that He has a purpose for all things, and is still the great God He has claimed to be.[51]

There is a temptation to get caught up in a belief that the time of seeing God's greatest glory has ceased. Perhaps we feel too old, too tired, or too weak in our beliefs. We may feel God's glory in our life was most evident during a season in which another individual was present in our life and now they are gone. While the changes of life and age can certainly be difficult, they are unavoidable. I had often resisted change both in my health, my friendships, and the direction of my life. Looking back, I am able to see things I couldn't see while in the midst of it all.

Aware that my words may have encroached upon your pain, your sadness, or a belief that you are of no use to God, please dear one; hear my intent. Let me say to you that God *is* working and He ***will*** continue to use your life if you will allow Him to have that freedom. It may not be in the same ways He has worked in the past and it isn't always easy; this I know. One thing is certain. He is able to accomplish far more than you can imagine regardless of your circumstances.[52] The challenge for every believer is to allow Him that freedom. An unrestrained faith allows God to work in His way, in His time, and for His purposes. This requires surrender of the

---

51 "For my thoughts are not your thoughts, and your ways are not My ways," (This is) the LORD'S declaration. "For as heaven is higher than the earth, so My ways are higher than your ways, and My thoughts than your thoughts." Isaiah 55:8-9 HCSB

52 Now to Him who is able to do above and beyond all that we ask or think – according to the power that works in you – to Him be the glory in the church and in Christ Jesus to all generations, forever and ever. AMEN – Ephesians 3:20-21 HCSB

way we think He should work or the way He should have done something in our lives. Would you allow God the opportunity to lead you as He did me, in a new way of following Him?

Surrendering to God's will for my life would mean that I had to release my own will. I desired a picture-perfect life. It was the one where my friends didn't die of disease while I lived and enjoyed God's healing. You see, I wanted all the joys and no sorrow. When I surrendered to His will, rather than mine, this became another turning point in my relationship with God. It is not that I became a person of greater faith, but rather because God had shown me unfailing love, great power, and that He was all He had claimed to be, He had become greater *in* me. Releasing myself and my will and surrendering to God's sovereignty was pivotal for me. I didn't have to live under guilt that my friends were gone and yet I lived. I no longer found it necessary to try and settle the score with God or understand why He had allowed things to transpire as they did. No longer angry or confused, I embraced Him in love all over again! I had peace in my heart that God was continuing to allow the circumstances around me to shape and grow my faith in Him. How wrong it would be for us to assume that this growing of our faith should only come out of joyful experiences. If we believe this then it is clear that we have read little of his Word. Those in whom God manifested his great power and whose accounts we have in scripture, lived lives marked by sacrifice, pain, sorrow, and sometimes even death. It is fact, whether we like it or not.

> True faith placed in something or someone is
> not really faith at all if our trust is expressed
> in only a fickle or sporadic way.

If my trust could only be placed in God during times of clear direction, or in times without risk or sadness, then what was the point? After all, was that really trust? I didn't want to be known as such a pathetic follower of Christ. Instead, I wanted to rise up in my faith in direct proportion to His revelation of Himself. The goal was never that I would be great. It was instead, that because God is great and in response to His activity, I wanted to exhibit great belief and faith. If His Word in my Bible is really truth, and I believe with all my heart it is, then I wanted to have the kind of faith that responded to that truth.

In each part of the journey of my life thus far, I had found God leading in ways that increased my faith and belief in Him. Now at this juncture,

I knew I was entering a new territory of exercising that faith. While I had never imagined many years before that God would show Himself so mightily in response to my feeble request to truly know Him, He had chosen to do just that. There was no way that I could have known that God would do such a dramatic work in my life both through the agony of disease and also the elation of healing. Likewise, I couldn't know that the painful loss of friends would be mixed with the sweet joy of endearing relationships that came about through these losses. We can never know all that our God knows and sees. This is where trust and faith in Him reaps great reward.

Now finding myself at a time of reflecting back, I realized that long before this juncture, my quiet times with God were spent questioning or requesting of Him rather than listening for Him. I remembered a decade earlier dramatically raising my outstretched Bible into the air, and boldly proclaiming in my prayer; "I believe you are the same God I read about in your Word. I believe I can know you just as powerfully as those I read about knew you." With all the faith I could muster, I sought to express a belief that sounded worthy of His revelation. I truly believed what I was saying and I wanted a deep relationship with Him. I really wanted to know Him in that same bold and mighty way I read about in my Bible.

Isn't it funny how we can pray such grandiose prayers having no idea just how seriously God takes our words? I was in no way a strong Christian possessing great faith, and I certainly was not one deserving of experiencing Him as the biblical Patriarch's did. I simply wanted to know Him in the most real way possible. Turns out, that's what God wanted as well. He looked upon my heart and knew how much I loved Him and truly wanted to experience Him. He heard my words and began working in my prayer life. I know this because He did what could only be attributed to Him.

> As I pray about a circumstance, God's power is never
> limited by any degree of difficulty I may perceive.

I entered a time that deepened my prayer life. I believe now that the one who seeks to truly know God in His power cannot have that experience apart from a prayer life that is equal to that pursuit. It's so easy for us to desire to see the evidence of God's power without the investment of time spent with him. I wanted God to change my scope of belief. I prayed to believe at all times that God was capable of accomplishing His purpose. I prayed that my perception of what God was able to do would be enlarged.

Then God revealed to me what the hindrance had been. It's so easy to find ourselves desiring greatness from our Lord and yet also harboring a disappointment in the outcome of things. I acknowledged through confession that I had limited God through my need to fully understand why He did as He chose to do. Along with my confession I acknowledged that my belief and trust in Him should not have ever been based upon my summation of His capabilities. I had things of great significance for which I was praying. I needed to learn to pray believing that God's power is never limited by any degree of difficulty I may perceive. As I prayed, I tried not to focus on the insurmountable evidence that could potentially erode my belief. Often we focus on all the negatives that project a picture of impossibility. My attitude had to change! I didn't need to know **how** God was capable, or **how** He would work it out. I only needed that small seed of faith that took Him at His Word. He Himself had stated that nothing was impossible for Him.[53] Either I truly believed this or I didn't. There could be no middle ground. This called for my routine response in any given situation to become, "God is capable." I was learning to truly believe and place my trust in who He said He was and what He claimed to be truth about Himself. It wasn't always easy and certainly there were times that I faltered, but God was showing me that He was worthy of trust.

While it seemed God was doing a new thing in continuing to grow my faith, I realized that it wasn't so new after all. He had in fact been at work strengthening my trust in Him through all the events of my life. I began to realize during times of reflection that God had always been working even in the times where I felt that my faith was at its weakest point. He had brought me through so many things; with each encounter, He met me in my weakness in order to be the strength within me. Throughout my life, He had built in me a stronger faith in Him. He had shown me new characteristics of who He was and how He could be trusted. Granted; the early part of my faith journey was not marked by huge steps of belief. Oftentimes God would work in the small and simple things of daily life. The faith I now saw emerging was one that was greater than I even realized I could enjoy. God has a unique way of leading us, even when we feel afraid to venture beyond what is familiar to us.

---

53 But Jesus looked at them and said, "With men this is impossible, but with God all things are possible." Matthew 19:26 HCSB

> Spending time reflecting on the memories of our journey
> of faith will allow us a fresh and new perspective of the
> revelation that God has previously given us of Himself.

The months spent working through the host of emotions following my healing and also Mike's death allowed me the opportunity to reflect back on the memories of my journey of faith. When we spend these times of reflection and quiet ourselves before God, it allows us to comprehend all that God has previously given us of Himself. We are then able to be renewed in our emotions rather than guided by them. It is God's revelation of Himself that guides us to hold to what we already have come to know of Him and also to soar on to new heights of belief and trust in Him.

Now as I reflected, allowing God to refresh my faith with the memories of earlier days in my faith journey, I settled in for a bit of a stay on one particular part of my early adventures in prayer. I wrapped my thoughts richly around this memory because it had been another pivotal turning point in my faith journey. It paralleled the place in which I now found myself at because it was such a mighty work of God that had seemed utterly impossible. Without doubt, it seemed vital for me to sojourn in this memory and draw strength from it.

Chapter Ten

Sharing the Unending Story

How the Power of One Life Affects another Life

Shortly after God led our family to move to the area where we now serve, I began to pray earnestly for a brother of mine. After marrying, attending seminary and serving in Ohio, we had lived away from family for over twenty years. During those years, the life of my brother Russell had taken a much different course than mine. My faith encompassed the activities of my life, and time was routinely spent with other Christians. Russell's activities encompassed a life built around his career as a beer salesman.

In the late sixties and in his teens, Russell had abandoned the idea of involving God or the church in his life. In his words, "Church was an institution of hypocrisy. It is a place where the deacons fight bitterly at church ball games but would then voice indignation when I wear jeans to church." Russell found easy acceptance from those who shared his same interest in beer, marijuana, and cars. That interest consumed him and his lifestyle, eventually leading him to quit high school and seek adventure.

Years later he met his wife and moved to her hometown on the Eastern Shore of Virginia. To Russell, life on the Eastern Shore seemed idyllic, especially later, when a daughter was born to them. However, drugs and partying still dictated his priorities. Russell acknowledged, "I loved my family, but I was lost both spiritually and emotionally." After struggling through job losses, a national beer distributor had given him newfound employment success and the partying persona fueled his ego. After fourteen years his already troubled marriage came to an end. He stated, "I began living with a friend who shared my addictive lifestyle, and he introduced me to his best friend, cocaine." Echoing Satan's hold on Russell, this supposed friend said, "Stick with me, and I will show you the world." He would soon discover the emptiness of that promise.

Russell now recalls, "While hosting a party with excessive alcohol and drugs, I found myself standing in the bedroom before a line of cocaine and staring into the mirror at the reflection of a lost soul. Somewhere deep within me there welled up a conviction within my soul. I began to call out to God." In a cry of helpless bondage he echoed, "Oh God, Satan has totally consumed me! I am powerless. If you don't intercede, I'm going to die!"

At this same time God had relocated my family near the area where Russell now lived. Just across the Chesapeake Bay, he was only an hour's drive from my home. I wanted to reconnect with him, yet I felt awkward in initiating a relationship after such a long time of separation. The awkwardness was due in part to the separation over time, but it was also felt because of the vast differences in the course of our adult lives.

I found myself at a time of great transition from our recent move. Having left behind all my friends, my longing for God's presence seemed even greater to me now, than in times past. I was actively involved in establishing a prayer ministry within our new church and these times in prayer had brought me to this place of praying, "God is capable." I began to pray for God to show me what to do and how He wanted to work in both Russell's life as well as my own.

Because we were in the fall season of Thanksgiving, I decided to host our extended family for the holiday. I prayed that God would bring Russell to our gathering, and God answered this prayer. While this answer to prayer didn't come in the same packaging I had envisioned, God did answer my prayer. On Thanksgiving Day a sales van with a huge beer logo pulled up and parked outside our home. I couldn't help but wonder if neighbors were talking about what was going on at the home of the new minister in town! I never asked Russell to move the van out of sight. Instead, I welcomed him with outstretched arms into a home of love, a place where hopefully he would feel anything but hypocrisy.

Russell remained for the meal, and then slipped away making arrangements to hook up with some friends and satisfy his addictions. While I didn't want him to leave, I knew he didn't need judgment or condemnation. Instead, I stood at the door asking him if I could pray for him before he left. As you can imagine, he was quite anxious to exit, and nervously fidgeted through my short prayer. It was some years later before I learned that he fidgeted while grasping the cocaine he had stored in his pocket. I told him to be safe and we would look forward to his return. The hours of the evening grew long as Russell's bed lay empty.

His return didn't come until the next day. Other family members had now left, and Russell and I were able to enjoy a genuine time of talking. We enjoyed sipping coffee while laughing over some old photographs. As we shared about our lives, there was a God-given openness as we discussed the differences in our lives. Russell said that he had prayed and he knew God was going to move. I was able to discuss the fear I felt for his lifestyle. He seemed to truly understand that my fears for him were based on love. Relaying to him how I had often wondered what it would take for God to get his attention, I was now able to comfortably talk with him about both my fears and also my desire to see him fulfill God's purpose for his life.

While Russell's words gave no evidence that he had considered God's need to take action for his attention, I could sense through the things we shared that God was working in his heart and attitude. The Lord used that conversation to allow me to see the glimmer of hope that would fuel the flames of my belief. This special time together increased my fervor in praying for change. I was able to continue to pray believing that God was capable of changing Russell's life. I began to pray as I never had before. There was a confidence and belief that I had not previously experienced. I believed not only that God *could* rescue Russell, but that He *would* do it.

Soon after he had been at my home, and following a three day binge of cocaine abuse, Russell left a bar where he had drunk excessively. Drinking all alone, completely intoxicated, he made the irresponsible decision to drive. He careened off the highway, hitting a concrete barrier at high speed. Sheering off the right side of his truck, his vehicle was totaled in an accident that should have claimed his life. Instead he left the hospital only badly bruised with stitches. The hospital attendant questioned him, "Who would you like us to call for you?" Stammering, Russell began, "That would be uh...call uh..." He realized how small his world had become. Later, while standing and cringing upon seeing his destroyed vehicle, he stated, "I knew then that God had moved and gotten my attention and wanted to intervene in my reckless life." He telephoned me, and I heard the words, "O.K., God has my attention!"

Russell never returned to the home of his professed friend. Moving from that rent-free luxurious beachfront home where his life had sunk into an abyss, he rented a small mobile home in a nearby trailer park. It was quite a contrast. All alone and with no real possessions, he sought to find a church where he felt he could reconnect with God.

Throughout our conversations, I could hear his intense apprehension and a fear that if he became involved in church, he would not be accepted. It was a small, everybody-knew-everybody town, and he was after all, still the beer man. God had made a change in his heart. Little could he, or any of us, realize the great changes that lay ahead. Isn't it wonderful how God accepts us right where we are in our lives? He didn't say to Russell, "You've got to get rid of that beer truck and then come to me!" He began the work in Russell's heart. God saw a bigger picture than only the beer truck. He saw a changed life.

> When surrounded by insurmountable
> negatives, one can always trust that God has
> knowledge of things mankind doesn't see.

During this time I continued to pray more fervently for Russell. I couldn't imagine that there were any Christians in his area because my only exposure had been his friends who lived similar lifestyles. As I prayed, I became profoundly led to trust that God had knowledge of things I couldn't see.[54] I asked God to put some Christians in his path.

Walking into a Baptist church, Russell entered and found a small older congregation at worship. He listened, prayed, and quietly slipped out prior to the end of the service. On a later visit a gentleman approached him showing interest in him. A relationship that was under God's leadership began. Russell lightheartedly states, "My sister, who had prayed for God to change my life, nearly lost hope that any Christians could be found in my town!" God had heard my prayers and already had His followers ready to be used by Him. The Lord brought believers into Russell's life from multiple directions and churches. These believers became Russell's life line of hope, encouragement, and spiritual understanding.

---

54 LORD, you have searched me and known me. You know when I sit down and when I stand up; you understand my thoughts from far away. You observe my travels and my rest; You are aware of all my ways. Before a word is on my tongue, You know all about it, LORD. You have encircled me; You have placed Your hand on me. This extraordinary knowledge is beyond me. It is lofty; I am unable to reach it. Psalm 139:1-6 HCSB

Throughout this journey he began to see God as he had never seen him before. First, it was in the faces of believers who were not condemning and then in the kindness of people who helped meet his needs.

While attending a faith-based retreat he had nervously agreed to be a part of, Russell met Jesus at a crudely erected wooden cross. He was invited to surrender to Jesus those things that hindered him from having a full relationship with God. Sometime earlier Russell had told the friend who had made this retreat possible, "I have done the church thing before. There is something missing in my life. Until I find out what it is, I will not make that commitment again." Now finding himself before the cross, and knowing that God was speaking into his heart, Russell scribbled on a piece of paper what he would later learn the apostle Paul called, "The thorn of the flesh."[55] Seeing those scribbled words, he began in his spirit to have an angry conversation with God. In his heart, he began to fight with God. "Why won't you move? I have done everything that I'm supposed to do! Why won't you give me what's missing?" Deep within his heart, the spirit of the Lord spoke back with the softest voice, "It's not what's missing, but it's what you have to give." In that moment Russell knew God was revealing what he had so long felt he was missing. While feeling intensely vulnerable, he also felt amazing peace. He knew God was saying, "You have to give all of yourself to me, dying to yourself so that I can raise you to new life. Then watch what I will do." In that moment Russell was no longer afraid to surrender. He was able to accept God in the fullness of His power and promises. While his life seemed as dark as the night, Russell moved out of the darkness toward the light of that crude cross. Grasping the hammer and nailing that paper to the cross brought Russell to his knees. Realizing that he could not continue in relationship with both God and this fleshly desire, he wept. Surrendering all of himself to God while at that crude cross, he entrusted himself into the Lord's amazing power. He states today, "It was the hardest most pivotal thing anyone can do." Russell prayed surrendering his life to Christ. He returned to his church and sought baptism. As pivotal and dramatic as this was, it was only the beginning. It was a transformation that was nothing short of a miracle. This was a power Russell was only beginning to experience.

As gripping as his addictions and lifestyle were, from that day forward God enabled him to walk away from the hold they had on his

---

55 Therefore, so that I would not exalt myself, a thorn in the flesh was given to me, a messenger of Satan to torment me so I would not exalt myself. 2 Corinthians 12:7 HCSB

life! Throughout Russell's transformation, God was growing my own faith and bringing His power into my prayer life. I could only stand in awe of the astounding change in Russell's life. It must at times be amusing to our God, as He hears our prayers expressing our faith and trust in Him. Then later He hears us profoundly amazed by His work. God answers our prayers, and hears us remark, "Can you believe that?" I think God is so patient and loving, that while He longs for us to express a confident belief that He will answer, He knows we can't fully grasp the greatness of His work in our lives. Surely He must be amused by us at times. Totally transformed, Russell realized that his new heart no longer had a passion for the beer-man persona that had once ignited his ego. God had changed his desires, the lifestyle that had once enslaved him, and also the addictions which no longer guided the direction of his life. He returned to school, received his GED, resigned his position in beer sales, and surrendered his life to serve God. Russell reflected, "I found myself packing up my few belongings at thirty-eight years of age and going away to college. I moved to Louisville, Kentucky, to attend college on a seminary campus. My life literally exploded into new areas of growth. I was free to become who God had made me to be."

There were a multitude of times throughout those years that God showed Himself, to Ray and I and also Russell. There was also the great host of family and friends that were a part of Russell's spiritual journey. There were so many needs he had that at times seemed overwhelming to all of us. The cost of tuition, housing, child support and also the task of studying were but a few of the challenges Russell faced. Separation from his daughter required great sacrifice an intense prayer. The purchase of a car for Russell to be able to drive to the local church where he served became a challenge for all of us to go deeper in our faith. As we prayed, God would use people we had never met to provide for needs and open opportunities for income. Russell's tuition was always fully paid through the sacrifice of many. Because he was so creative in the design of his dorm room, it was used to give tours to potential students, thereby reducing the cost of his rent. He was able to find work that always enabled his child support payments to be made. Clothing was freely given to him through a clothes closet donation center on the campus. Care packages arrived from believers he didn't even know. It was an example of the early New Testament church. People even sold items of value in order that Russell would have what was needed. Amazingly, God even made it possible for him to acquire a car for only five dollars through a dealership promotional. This promotional required the purchaser to be sitting in a specific car at a specific moment. In God's timing Russell was sitting behind the wheel of the five dollar car at just the right moment.

God has both a heavenly host of angels to work at his command and He also has a human host. This human host is His church. It is those who believe in Him and are willing to make their lives and possession's available for His use. It is the one who doesn't cling to his own life and possessions, but instead listens for God to lead him outside of himself. It is the individual who looks outside the walls of their local church and offers his time, resources and talents to be Christ in the world. For us, God was working in the lives of many believers who would respond in just this way. Clearly, God was deepening the faith of all of us as we prayed, asked of Him, and then sat astounded at these answers to our prayers.

Finally, the celebration of Russell's graduation was shared by a host of many believers who had shared the journey with him. A group of women who had often sent care packages even purchased a suit for him to wear to his graduation ceremony. What joy it was for Russell to also share this day with his daughter! He had experienced the wonderful visits with her throughout his time in Kentucky, and he ultimately led her to know God as he did. Through tears he exclaimed, "What joy it was for me to be the one to baptize my daughter and to also have both her, and the lady who would be my future wife beside me on graduation day." Yes, God had led Russell to serve in a congregation during his college education, and it would be in this very church that God introduced him to his future wife.

Following graduation and returning to Virginia, Russell would later find himself in the pulpit of the very same church he had quietly slipped into on that dark night so long ago. This same church had baptized him, recommended him to school, and had later ordained him. While Russell had found employment through a newly formed Boys & Girls Club, he knew this was but a stepping stone as he sought what God would have for him in the tiny town of Cape Charles. Soon the tiny church that had such great impact on his life found themselves in need of a pastor. Likewise, Russell found himself in need of a church where he could serve. As Russell said, "Only God could have brought us together in the way He did!" The church voted to have him come on staff as their pastor, and he has served this congregation for nearly ten years.

Because of the amazing way only God can transform a life, many others have come through the doors of this church and found a lifeline of hope, just as Russell did and countless others have found. The church that had less than 20 people attending when God led him to their pastorate now fills their building with five times that number of people. They have added staff members, expanded ministries, purchased additional properties for further growth, and taken mission trips. Their building currently houses a Hispanic church ministering to the needs of local migrant workers. While each of these ministries is celebrated, they come with the challenge for this congregation to deny themselves and allow God to lead. Is all of this because of Russell? Certainly not! It is because of the mighty God who is the only one who can transform a life in such a way that it becomes a beacon of hope and power.

As I reflect, I think about my own amazing journey. I consider the times that seemed impossible, not only in Russell's life, but in my own. I also consider how God has increased my faith and strengthened my belief in who He is and all He is capable of doing. No one can really know the fullness of that capability. It is truly infinite. Yet, we are invited to experience His capabilities.

> One can never know the full extent of what one
> expression of faith or selfless act for God will accomplish.

In my own journey with God, I have found that often He is answering our prayers in a way of His choosing. I believe this is so that He is able to work in both my life and also the lives of others. It is true, one never knows the extent of what one expression of faith or selfless act for God will accomplish. I have learned to consider my words as I pray. Can we really pray asking God to meet a need, while being unwilling to make whatever personal sacrifices we are able to make in order to join God in His work? Confronting this question made me more aware of how often I prayed for God to meet a particular need while not considering the role I played. Sometimes God has orchestrated our involvement in another's life for the very purpose of being a part of providing answers to the prayers of others. In praying for my brother Russell, I grew so much through the joy of sacrifice and the blessing of giving. Throughout my experiences with Russell I had asked great things of God. I had learned to pray with greater belief. One of the sweetest blessings of it all has been to know how God allowed me to take part in His work. What a privilege this is, and yet how often do we forsake it?

All too often I might know God has answered prayer, and therefore believe I can cease that request and move on. All the while, I might never realize how God is still working and bringing good out of those prayers. Our prayers are like investments that guarantee growth. This investment of prayer is not controlled by a fickle stock market, but instead held under the guidance of an unchanging and powerful God who is always in control.[56] He is able to move in our favor and act on our behalf even when it seems unlikely to us. The Holy Spirit guides us as we pray.[57] What a blessing this is for us!

I could never have imagined how God would involve Himself in my prayer life while at the same time change the life of my brother. Now finding myself reflecting some years later, not only upon Russell's journey but also my own, I faced the pivotal question. What would God have me to do with my healing, the loss of friends, and the direction of my life? I now had the challenge of continuing on with Him. I had seen God work in so many amazing ways. The months of reflection, prayer, and meditating on my great God had healed some hurting places in my heart. It had also ignited a passion once again for not waning in my faith. I wanted all the more to find His purpose for it all, both the joys and the sorrows. I knew God had done great things in my life, and also in my brother's life. I knew He had brought about both of our healings for His eternal purpose. It, no doubt, had been a way He had shown His transforming power to a watching world. I had seen His purpose being fulfilled in Russell's life and knew that it was now time for me to step out and bring action to what I knew God was saying to me. Sometimes the prospect of taking action is frightening to us. We don't know what that action will look like. Even more frightening, we don't know the cost or what we might have to sacrifice. It is completely unchartered territory. While we love God and enjoy the relationship with Him, we sometimes prefer to just keep praying and not get too involved.

Even before my healing occurred, I had been speaking in churches, leading women's retreats, and enjoying a host of opportunities to share about the awesome God that is ours if we only accept Him. I knew God was leading me to step out in faith, leave my full-time job and serve Him.

---

56 This God, our God for ever and ever - He will lead us eternally. Psalm 48:14 HCSB

57 In the same way the Spirit also joins in our weakness; because we do not know what to pray for as we should, but the Spirit Himself intercedes for us with unspoken groaning's. And He who searches the heart knows the mind-set, because He intercedes for the saints according to the will of God. Romans 8:26-27 HCSB

Throughout my time of prayer about this, He had used so many avenues to make Himself known. His own spoken Word in my Bible and messages through pastors and teachers had confirmed over and over again. He was calling me to follow Him. I asked Him to not only show me His will but to show me clearly, and He did just that.

Sometimes I find myself praying to God, asking for direction or confirmation. Then when He answers, I want to back up and question again. I want to ask Him to show it to me again in a different way. Repeating this process over time, finally God allowed a circumstance to occur in such a way that I knew within my spirit: I was at a crossroads with God. It was the place of response on my part. It was no longer a time for asking, but a time for action. God knew the thoughts and intent of my heart.[58] His desire was to hear and answer my prayers, but He also expected action from me as He led in response to my prayers.

My prayers may sound as if I want an answer, but then as God gives me one, I want to keep asking until it seems to fit into my belief box. During the time I was praying about leaving my employment and serving Him full-time, I had two boys preparing to leave for college in just a matter of months. There was also the reality that the health insurance for my family was through my employment. I deeply wanted to continue this journey of faith God had traveled with me, but I was terrified at the prospect of leaving my career. There seemed to be insurmountable evidence that was all around me as though it were screaming out, "It's not possible!" Surely you must be thinking, "How can she question God? Look at all He has done in her life up until this time." You are certainly justified in asking. Isn't it just an unspeakable blessing that God continues to work with us?

It was at this crossroad that God helped me determine just how serious I was about believing and trusting Him. This time in my faith journey became an altar of sacrifice. It was the place where I would either choose to submit to God's leadership, claim belief and trust in Him, or do battle with Him. I battled with God as I expressed my doubts and fears without ever surrendering that fear. If I were not putting action to my belief in who He was and what He was able to do, could I really say that I trusted Him with the outcome? I knew God had spoken and I desired to place my trust once again in what I could not see visibly. Surrendering my fears, I resigned my position and founded *Faith Steps*, an organization committed

---

58 For the Word of God is living and effective and sharper than any two-edged sword, penetrating as far as to divide soul, spirit, joints, and marrow; it is a judge of the ideas and thoughts of the heart. Hebrews 4:12 HCSB

to serving and ministering to women. I wanted more than anything to help others to grow in their faith and allow God to reveal Himself to them. The opportunity to speak at women's events led to further avenues of ministry. I began hosting women's events and retreats where women would get away, be pampered and prepared to know God in the realness of who He truly is. Quarterly, I would host evenings of fellowship with small dessert socials. What woman doesn't love a dessert buffet? I would welcome women to take a break out the business of life and I'd share the comedic life of a character I created named, "Precious Pearl." These evenings allowed women to laugh with Pearl and relate to the realities of being women in a hectic world. Laughing at the realities of marriage, mothering, the workplace and maintaining our bodies allowed these ladies to connect with one another. Then I was able to close these evenings with the truth that they are loved just as they are and that God wanted to walk with them through their journey of life, even with all its challenges. There are now 150 women attending these evening events. Since leaving my employment, there have been no regrets and no looking back. Our sons have both completed college and they, along with our daughter, have married and brought the incredible joy of grandchildren into our lives. Challenges have come and gone, as they do for everyone, yet God has been faithful, just as He promises He will be.[59]

God never ceases to amaze me and often in ways that take my breath away. One such moment brings me to the conclusion of our time spent together in this book. Five years after the formation of my ministry, I was speaking at a women's retreat for a local church. Donna, the pastor's wife, was a friend of mine. While there, she and I were conversing and catching up on each other's lives and families. Having fought a host of interruptions and delays in getting to the retreat, she'd been late arriving that evening. Donna had a group of women around her as she relayed to me how she would have turned around and gone back home except that she had brought a young woman with her. She went on to say that this woman simply had to meet me. Startled by her statement, I questioned, "Why me?" Donna went on to explain that when I met the woman and heard her story, I would know why she had fought such a battle to get this dear lady to the retreat. Overwhelming curiosity consumed me. I couldn't imagine why this individual would want to meet me, so I blurted out, "Go and find her. Bring her to me now, I'm anxious to meet her!"

---

59 God, who has called you into fellowship with his Son Jesus Christ our Lord, is faithful. I Corinthians 1:9 NIV

She left and within minutes returned with a very kind, smiling woman whom she introduced as Sherrie. She seemed anxious to meet me and I was equally anxious to hear her story. I was not a recognizable name by any means, so I couldn't imagine why she wanted to meet me. Donna left us to ourselves as Sherrie and I tucked away in the corner of a large conference room. Once we positioned ourselves away from the crowd, she began to tell me why she had come to meet me. It was unforgettable and truly a God appointment between the two of us.

Her God story unfolded as she shared with me that she was from the same town where my brother Russell lived. She had grown up there and had been involved in the same drug scene that had enslaved Russell years ago. As a young adult she had become a mother and could see the destructive effects of her addictive lifestyle. She wanted more for her daughter and had chosen to leave the area in hopes of making a better life for both of them. Sherrie had no plans of including church in her pursuit of a better life. Just like Russell, she had experienced the hypocrisy of the church and wanted no part of that. She had moved across the bay and now lived in a housing complex that was adjacent to the area where Donna and her husband had recently planted a church. It didn't have the trappings of a church as they were meeting in a rented school building.

At that time their church was busy promoting a summer camp for youth. They had distributed flyers in the complex where Sherrie lived. She relayed how she had no money for extra activities and decided that perhaps this would be a way she could enrich her daughter's life without financial cost. With great apprehension she walked over to the parking lot where they were registering for the camp. When she got there, Russell was standing behind one of the tables. He had recently graduated from Bible college and returned home. The new church plant had just begun and needed additional summer staff. The church had employed him to lead in their summer youth programs. Sherrie relayed how she had looked intently at Russell just as he did at her. At this point in my conversation with her, she leaned in towards me and her entire demeanor changed. In her own words she stated, "He was the first real Jesus I had ever seen." Then she went on to explain.

In years past Sherrie had partied and drugged often with Russell. She relayed how she had been with Russell at times when he was no longer able to get home; she would drive him home and help him into his house. She had been part of his partying and participated in that vicious cycle of life. Having experienced believers who offered much judgment and little love, she had left that town, only returning for an occasional funeral. She had lost all contact with Russell. The only image she had of him was the one she had left behind. It was that of the beer salesman who was a drinking and drugging partner. She knew his marriage had ended but she had lost contact and knew nothing more of him.

Now she found herself face to face with him and nothing about what she saw lined up with the image she had held in her mind. "Russell" she stammered, "Is that really you?" He was equally surprised to see her. Laughingly he said, "Yes, it's me...but then again, it's not me." He then went on to tell her the greatest story one can ever tell another. It's the ageless tale of how God can change a life. He relayed to her how God had done that for him.

Now nestled in the corner of that room, Sherrie shared with me how Russell had told her of that Thanksgiving Day when he had come across the bay in hopes of reconnecting with his sister. He shared with her about the prayer that had been prayed at my door and of the subsequent accident. She knew every detail of how God had worked in his life. She fixed her eyes on mine and emphatically stated, "It was the first time I truly believed I could trust *this* Jesus, not the one I had rejected, but the One that stood before me in the life of a friend who was undeniably and forever changed." She said it took some time for her, but she eventually surrendered her life to God.

"I came here to meet you," were her words. "You may think what you did in praying for your brother Russell was only about him. I have come to tell you that it changed my life. I have come to thank you and to tell you that it is my desire to serve you this weekend." Oh, dear one, as I write I can't even begin to form any words that would be worthy of such an expression of the greatness of our God. Only He could weave a thread of His love and tender mercy, knitting the hearts of believers together, in the way only He can do!

Sherrie spent the entire weekend standing back in the shadows, ever present and always serving me. Her words were few. Her acts of service were great. Sometimes it was a cup of water. Other times it was the gathering of my materials. All seemed like a simple task to the casual observer, but it was monumental to me. I was so humbled by her assistance and most of all her loving spirit of servant-hood. When it was time for me to go home, she was the last person waiting for me beside my car. She had packed some of my materials and carried them to the car for me. She stood beside my door as I hugged her and told her how she had been sent to me by God.

What Sherrie didn't realize was that prior to this retreat I had prayed fervently for God to give me very clear and specific guidance regarding the ending of this book. Having met her that weekend, I knew God would have all of us to be reminded of a central truth of His. When in relationship with God, the story never ends. What God is doing in your life today is preparation for tomorrow. His work in your life and in response to your prayers becomes His way of living His glory and power through you. It is seen by a watching world. It is truly the only way our faith in this glorious God will have any effect on the lives of a world that God loves. I chose not to abandon my faith. I wanted then, just as I do now, to allow the God who chooses to live out His glory through me to have all of me. I want my faith like fire to consume the dross of a mundane belief system and instead cause the world to see that He really is who He claims to be: The Living God. He is worthy of every bit of my trust!

My friend, we have come to the end of this book and our time together, but certainly not the end of the story. Oh, how I have enjoyed sharing part of the journey with you. As I have shared the story of my life, I've prayed that you'll be challenged to consider how God is working in your life and that you would now go share your story. As you go, let me leave you with this encouragement. Live richly and deeply in the presence of God. Don't waste a minute given to you. Take the time to notice those whom God puts in your path. You are always a part of someone else's story and with God this has great value.